Annie's Story

A Childhood in the North of England
1923–1942

by

Anne Wilde

Acknowledgements

To Simon and Kristine with many thanks for their invaluable help in preparing my manuscript.

To Hannah, Thomas and Benjamin who may one day, have interest in the family story.

To Jim for sharing our past and for his useful suggestions.

To my cousin Edna who, although she may not have known it, gave me the impetus to press ahead with publication.

To the Maltese island of Gozo, our home for seven happy years and where our friends still live. It was there, in the peace of our last hot summer that I finished the book.

British Library Cataloguing in Publication Data.
A catalogue record for this book is available from the British Library.

© 2002 Anne Wilde

Anne Wilde asserts the moral right to be identified as the author of this work.

ISBN 0 9544005 0 X

Published by Anne Wilde
18 Walkington Road, East Yorkshire, HU20 3UT
Telephone (01482) 876638
E.mail: a.wilde@amserve.com

Printed by Highgate Print Limited
4 Newbegin, Beverley, HU17 8EG. Telephone (01482) 886017

Preface

THIS STORY is centred round my life as a very young child and set in the twenties and thirties. It is presented through the mind of a quiet, rather solitary little girl, born in the North of England.

I was able to recall quite easily the most mundane of events because, somehow, they seemed of significance. The only amendments I made were in the conversations and I have written an approximation of what people said, even though I could not remember all the exact words. Although I can by no means claim that this account is a historical document, it does hint of changes and development far beyond my own small world.

It also suggests enormous differences between the various levels of society. The 'class system', much reviled in Britain, was certainly in existence then, but did not affect me at all. I was vaguely aware of the 'Toffs' at the top of the scale and people living in the abject poverty of city slums at the bottom. I suppose that my family could have been labelled as 'Working Class' and as I grew older I realised that I was expected to climb out of it one day, by means of education and choice of profession. But I didn't really care. Maybe I thought about it once, when by mother showed me her wedding photograph.

'Why didn't you have a white dress with a veil and lots of bridesmaids?', I asked.

'Couldn't afford it. That's why!' was mother's curt reply.

'And where are your flowers? Brides always have flowers!'

'Didn't have any!' she said.

My secure and unchallenged childhood must appear, to the present generation, like life on a backward planet! The changes came, but very slowly and my life was not significantly different from that of my own parents. But they, of course, lived through two wars. Myself only one.

Communication changed the most. We relied on letters and visitings, with long gaps in between, not on the instant messages of phone and computer. Nor did we travel so far, nor so fast.

We lived our lives by unspoken rules, moral or practical and based on necessity. There were things which were 'done' and those which were 'not done'. Wearing a hat and gloves, going to Sunday School was what you did; but washing clothes on Sunday was not in the rule book!

Marriage and family ties were strong. We lived in close communities, in the streets of terraced houses, with neighbours who would help anyone in need. Thus in retrospect, we know that the re-housing in high-rise flats, when people were separated, seriously eroded the unity of family life.

But in my own home, peace and security seemed always there. The ghastly events in other countries would, I thought, never happen in mine. Until 1939!

Life was good. If in our city streets we could play freely and if in our parks we could run about without harm, what more did we need! There was no-one in my life who analysed the whys and the wherefores. I accepted things as they were and expected them to last forever.

Contents

Annie and Mother and Father in stiff collar.

that time and they used to shine silver in the rain. The clip-clop of horses' hooves were heard every day down our street. First there was the milkman's brown horse pulling a cart with the milk churns, then the dark heavy horse which came with the coal-man and also the poor bony creature which belonged to the rag-and-bone man, my favourite, because he looked so lonely.

The houses opposite were exactly like ours, the only difference, being perhaps, a plant standing stiffly on the front room window sill. There was rarely any sight of the occupants for, like us, people lived their lives at the back, saving the Sunday parlours for when the visitors came. In those front rooms, if you were lucky enough to own a fine table or even a piano, the legs would be wrapped around with thick woolly stockings in case of damage. But it was in the kitchen where they would eat, work, quarrel perhaps, and deal with naughty children. On Fridays they would count their wages on the wooden table.

Our front door, with its number nine, opened into a hallway with a flight of stairs and led into the back kitchen and its tiny scullery. There was another small room which contained my father's roll-top desk which used to open and close with a loud clatter. I loved that desk with its piles of papers and all the intriguing cubby holes (and one secret drawer) where father kept his bottles of red and blue ink, rulers and pens with pointed metal nibs.

He had once worked in a cotton-mill in the small town where he lived, but seeing no possibility of a future there, he learned other skills and moved to the city to become a clerk in an office just a short walk away from Alexandra Grove. Mother used to stay at home all day, as all wives did and never went out to work after she married. Women, once married usually had to leave their jobs, so that the main work force was maintained by men. Those who did keep a job were paid very little – no equal pay in those days!

So it was father who was responsible for earning the money to support the three of us (I remained an only child). I remember that he earned two pounds a week, later increasing to three and then, when I was older, it became five. I was told that he had a 'white-collar' job and that was correct I knew, because he always wore a stiff white collar which he fastened to his shirt with a stud. Sometimes the collar would coil round his neck and spring about. The he would lose the pearly stud and he used to search for it on the floor, getting angrier by the minute. I wondered how he could wear such an uncomfortable thing which dug into his neck and made a red mark. Every week, the soiled collars were put into a cardboard box and given to the laundry man who returned them the following week, shiny and white and stiffer then ever. Father never seemed to mind.

He used to walk home for his dinner at quarter past five, so that meal times rarely varied. Sometimes he wore his bowler hat and sometimes his trilby. Once he walked in with a letter poked into his hat band which he had forgotten to post. We thought it was very funny.

The money which my father gave to my mother each Friday was divided up and put away very carefully. She had two glass jars labelled RENT and GAS in which she put several coins, while the rest went into her black purse with its several compartments. One section was for coppers – pennies, ha'pennies and farthings. The silver went into another – threepenny bits, sixpences, florins and half-crowns. Very occasionally there was a crinkly brown ten-shilling note printed with the heads of King George and Queen Mary. (We usually called it a ten-bob note). The success of this management was mainly due to the juggling and scheming of my mother, in order, as she said, 'to make ends meet.'

That black purse of my mother's stayed with her during the whole of my childhood and it became almost as important to me as it was to her. I became almost identified with it and with whatever financial condition it was in. I worried that one day she might open her purse and find nothing in it! If it was becoming rather empty I would sigh as she did and wait anxiously for Friday's pay-day. I learned very early that life could not go on without money!

When visitors arrived, the money in her purse would go down alarmingly and mother had to conjure up all sorts of schemes which often meant buying less, or doing without things herself. But she never in her life borrowed money for housekeeping or clothes.

'I'll do without first,' she would say, or, 'It'll do a bit longer' as she mended holes in a jumper or put a patch on father's sleeve where he had leaned on his desk. She turned collars round on shirts and blouses and sat with a wooden toadstool darning holes in our socks. My dresses were let down at the hems as I grew.

She herself, both in summer and winter, wore a dark cotton dress, on top of which she tied her bibbed apron – her pinny as she called it. Her shoes were always shabby. It was father who had the best ones because he had to walk to work. He once tried re-soling a shoe on a borrowed last but he was not of a practical nature and it was considered a failure!

Mother brought her groceries at the 'Corner Shop' except on days when she went to the local market which she loved. Sometimes she would buy an odd cup or saucer in her favourite Willow Pattern, even if it had a slight chip on one side or a flaw in its decoration.

'It won't show,' she would say 'And it's cheap enough.'

She knew a poem about the willow pattern and sometimes, after tea, if I felt she was in a good mood, I would ask her to repeat it.

> 'Two swallows flying high,
> A little vessel sailing by
> A bridge with three men, if not four,
> A weeping willow hanging o'er.
> There is the castle where it stands,
> Facing the church with all its lands.
> A tree with many apples on
> And there's the fence that ends my song.'

'Right! That's it!' she would say. 'It's time to do the washing up. You dry the saucers and don't drop any!'

'I'd rather wash!' I would plead, thinking of those lovely mounds of bubbles I could plunge may hands into.

'Not likely!' she would reply 'I'm more careful with the soap!'

Mother was always first up every morning. Father would follow and I would be the last, although I was often wakened early by the milk man. I would hear his clopping horse and the lids rattling on the milk churns. Sometimes I jumped out of bed in order to see the brown horse standing so patiently, his breath steaming in the chilly air. I wondered if he felt the cold and I thought it would be nice if he had a blanket on his back. My mother might make him one, I thought, knowing perfectly well what her answer would be!

'What! Make a blanket for a horse! As if I haven't enough to do! Not enough hours in the day, in this house!'

I saw the two big wheels on the cart and the two big churns, as mother went to the door with her jug and its lace cover. She watched intently as he used his measure to fill her jug.

'One pint missus! Good morning to you!'

Then the horse would toss its head and move on.

I would look across the street to see if anything of interest was happening. A few people would be moving about and Mrs Smith already sweeping her step. Snowy her cat used to edge himself out through the open door and come over to us. Mother wasn't too fond of him and I would see him flicking off under the privet hedge. The wind would always be there, blowing dead leaves and the chimney smoke, for fires would all be lit. If it blew smoke sideways that would mean a bad day – straight up and it would be fine. Sometimes I used to imagine that not only the sparrows lived up there among the chimney pots, but also little people called Quirks and Querns who used to jump from roof to roof.

It was after breakfast of porridge and thick white toast that father would set off for work. When I heard the clock strike eight I would listen for the door to bang and a minute later there he would be, in his trilby hat, walking down the street towards the busy main road where the trams went by.

When he came to the corner I knew that he would be passing those other houses, bigger than ours, fronted by bushes and sparse trees, behind spiky railings in need of paint. He would pass Quilligotti's, a name that was quite wonderful to repeat over and over again. They used to cut large chunks of shiny stone there but what they were used for I never really knew. I wished I had a name like Quilligotti.

He would soon be passing that other interesting building with the many windows, which looked blind and lifeless. A very high wall enclosed it and a tall wooden gate, which father said was kept firmly locked. 'How can people get out!' I asked, but nobody ever explained. Perhaps there was nobody there at all.

'I think they have all died', I said to mother, one day, as we walked past it ourselves.

'Who?' she said.

'All those people who used to live in that big house'.

'They still live there. They are all sisters and they help the poor'.

'It must be a very big family', I said.

They couldn't have been very tall either, because there was a board at one end which, mother said, told us quite plainly who they were, 'Little Sisters of the Poor'. Then one day I saw a little sister looking very stern in a long black dress down to her ankles, a silver cross and a wide hat with wings that dipped as she walked. She had white bandages round her chin and I saw that she was indeed quite small.

I pulled at mother's hand. 'Where is she going?' I asked.

'To feed the poor'

'What with?'

'Rich people will give her money and she will use it to buy food'. I could not imagine why people had no food, I thought it was a dreadful state of affairs. I pulled at mother's hand to make her stop.

'Shall we knock on the gate?'

'What for?'

'Well we can tell them that we'll come back with some bread'.

'Not today!' The subject seemed closed and I felt sorry that we couldn't help.

'Has she got a name that lady? That lady with wings on her head'
'She's a nun and she loves God'.
'Oh', I said and there seemed nothing else to add.

I was remembering all this as I stood at the window. Father had long disappeared and no one else was about. I felt my feet getting colder, so I picked up my clothes and trotted downstairs. Then I warmed myself by the lovely kitchen fire with its flames leaping up towards the back chimney and the kettle singing on the hob.

Once a week, on a Monday, mother had a wash – day, which was not my favourite occupation, nor hers, I think. This was because we had to go down into the cellar which shut out most of the light. A little window was only just above the ground outside and so the sun never had a chance to creep in. Everything smelled dark and musty. It was cold and clammy with its old brick walls and moist flag-stoned floor. There was a square brick boiler in one corner and a large wash-tub with a posser. This was a circular shape of wood attached to a central pole and two side-pieces, which you held as you plunged it up and down in the soapy water. I tried to use it but it was too strong for me and it wouldn't help me at all, so I left that job to mother with her strong arms. An old mangle stood nearby with its large wheel and two wooden rollers to squeeze out the water. But that was heavy too and very difficult to turn. Mother worked really hard on wash days.

There was, however, much satisfaction when the clothes were washed and pegged out on the line outside, where they fought with the wind, flapping with a cracking sound. But we all hated it when it was raining and the damp clothes had to be hauled up to the ceiling on a wooden rack, so that everything got steamy and took so long to dry. There were days too, in the winter when the washing dried stiff in the frosty air and fathers shirts looked like scarecrows on the line.

After hours of washing we always needed a drink. 'Let's have a brew Annie! Go and get the mugs'.

The kettle would now be boiling on the trivet close to the flames. It was very important that kettle, and it remained on duty all day long, providing water for the pans, the teapot, the washing up bowl and for washing our hands in the scullery (also my dirty knees). It was also pressed into service when I had my weekly dip in the old tin bath in front of the fire, one of my great delights, and of childhood itself. Never to be forgotten was the feeling of security and wellbeing, as, wrapped in a big white towel, and smelling of soap, I was dusted like a cake with talcum powder!

When mother made tea, she put fresh tealeaves at the bottom of a mug and poured on the boiling water where they swirled madly round before settling on the bottom. Once, when I was three, my mother accidentally knocked a cup of boiling water on to my foot. It hurt and I thought that my foot was on fire. We both cried, mother and me, and then she put brown ointment on it, with a long bandage. It still hurt. When father came home, he was upset too. But the next day the fire in my foot had died down and then, after a time, a huge blister formed, leaving a red patch which stayed with me for years.

After our morning brew of tea, it would be time to go to the corner shop. Mother would put on her old black coat and a hat, which came right down over her ears.

'Let's put on your coat,' she said, one wintry day. 'We'll fasten it well because the wind isn't half cold! You'd better wear your scarf too'.

It was a beautiful scarf, knitted with really soft wool and it had deep fringes at each end. It was put round my neck, crossed over my chest and knotted at the back. I had a pair of gloves too, secured with elastic to my coat sleeves and I felt all bundled and cosy, ready for any old wind.

The shop was a short walk away and I carried the empty basket. The lady who owed the shop was Mrs. Hunt and I think there was a Mr. Hunt too, but I never saw him.

'Has she any children?' I asked, as we hurried along. Mother shook her head, as if she didn't like talking in the wind.

The shop door stood at an angle on a corner and had two large windows full of tins and packets, with posters stuck onto the glass. Nuggett's Shoe Polish, Drummer Dyes, Coleman's Mustard, Chiver's Marmalade, Rowntree's Cocoa and MacKintosh's Toffee. Inside there was an interesting smell of all sorts of things mixed up together. There were great sacks of flour, with wooden scoops, large bags of sugar and big square tins containing biscuits. A large tea-chest, lined with silver paper was labelled Mazawattee tea, or so my mother said.

THE EVER WELCOME CUP

Solace and satisfaction are always to be found in a cup of really good tea. Get them in full measure by insisting on

MAZAWATTEE
The Quality TEA

I loved that word, so I pulled her sleeve and said very seriously, 'Don't forget the Mazawattee tea'. They laughed and I was pleased because I think mother would have forgotten it if I had not reminded her.

There was row upon row of tins on shelves and, hanging from the ceiling, were buckets, mops, brushes, bundles of strong smelling fire lighters and some very nasty looking fly paper.

The best thing in the shop was an enormous mound of golden yellow butter on the counter.

'Half a pound of best butter', said mother. Mrs. Hunt cut off a block and then proceeded to use the two wooden butter pats to make it into a nice shape. She was a bit rough I thought but I quite liked the sound, slap! bang! slap! Then the butter was placed on to a piece of paper and put onto the scales. They fascinated me, with a piece of metal on one side to put the butter on and a piece at the other side for the weights, so shiny that I could see part of my face reflected there, all stretched and out of shape. I put out my tongue at myself,

'Stop it!' said mother crossly.

'Half a pound exactly!' said Mrs. Hunt.

My mother's basket now contained, along with the butter, a crusty loaf of bread, a neat white parcel of tea, a brown paper bag with biscuits and a stiff blue one with sugar inside. I think she had some bacon but I didn't like to see it sliced so I had turned my head away.

'You've forgotten something Annie!' said Mrs. Hunt, as we turned to go.

It was a little sweet; all pink on the outside, but it would turn all colours if I sucked away the layers.

'What do you say?' reminded mother.

'Thank you,' I said politely.

'Save it until you get home.'

When we left the shop, mother stopped to speak to Mrs. Smith, but we soon hurried on to keep warm, in the direction of home. We passed the street corner where the Hurdy-Gurdy man sometimes used to be.

'He's not here today,' said mother. 'Too cold for his little monkey.' I slowed down. 'Don't drag your feet. Come on!' She hurried on.

I loved the Hurdy-Gurdy with its black velvet covered box on wheels and a large handle, which produced music when it was turned. Odd music it was, coming out with a kind of wheeze and it seemed to match the dark faced man with curly hair escaping from under his cap. Sometimes, but not always, he brought his monkey, fastened to the Hurdy-Gurdy by a chain. I was never happy about that chain and wished it could be free. I hoped that the man looked after it and gave it nuts. It had two large sad eyes.

Back home, there was a whole afternoon of exciting things to do and I cannot remember ever being bored. My mother, never one to sit doing nothing, always had several projects in hand. She never relaxed, or read a book, nor did she ever pick up the Manchester Guardian which my father brought in sometimes, and although she had her 'People's Friend', I never recall her reading it.

'What are we going to do now?' I said, when we reached our warm kitchen.

'A cup of tea for me. Milk for you' said mother.

'After, can I help to wind your wool?' I asked. Knitting wool, in those days came in long hanks and had to be wound into balls, so that a small pair of hands, outstretched came in very useful. I would watch the woollen strand turning itself over in my right hand and twisting its way to my left, until it finally criss-crossed itself into a large coloured ball.

One day, after a long talk with father and after a visit to the Post Office where she had a few shillings put by, she bought a knitting machine from a lady who had no further use for it. With great excitement, mother set it up in the kitchen, which cut down the little space we had, even more. I was fascinated by its rows of tiny needles, the weights which hung down below it and the little oil can. I pressed it and a dribble of oil came out.

'Put that down!' said mother 'And don't touch it again!'

When she was knitting I can remember the zizzing sound it made. Zizz-zizz, zizz-zizz. But what a clutter there was in the kitchen, with hanks of wool, a winding frame like a big umbrella, and all the patterns. There were the days when mother broke her rules. The meals were late, but the garments multiplied all winter – jumpers, scarves and woolly hats. In those days wool was cheap.

If she wasn't knitting, she would be sewing on her treadle machine, surrounded by cottons, shuttles, pins and scissors. She used to draw her own patterns on brown paper, carefully measured with a long stick ruler marked in inches. I always had at least one pretty dress and often she would unpick a garment of her own to make into a skirt for me. Sometimes she would make a coat out of thick cloth and would use a heavy iron called a Goose which was put to heat near the fire. It was used to press seams with a damp cloth making hisses and bursts of steam.

Sometimes she would need to go up into the attic to fetch Dolly, a strange object shaped like a plump lady, upon whose curves she would pin her material pieces and her pattern, in order to check the fit. She would often talk with a few pins in her mouth and instructed me never to copy such a bad habit.

As a special treat I would be allowed to go with her up to the attic, going gingerly ahead of her with an admonitions not to be careless and fall down the steep stairs again. The attic had a woody, closed-in smell of its own and there was dust and several cobwebs. A tiny pane of glass was set in the ceiling, not too useful because of all the soot from the rooftop. The attic was used, mother said, for storing junk.

'What's junk?' I would ask.

'Rubbish. Junk is rubbish.'

'But if it's rubbish, why do you keep it?'

'Because you should keep things for a rainy day'.

Why was a rainy day different from a sunny one, I wondered. But if all this was junk then I quite liked it and resolved to have some of my own one day. There were piles of old boxes, suitcases, umbrellas with broken spokes, some tattered old books and several pairs of shoes.

'They can be mended one day!' said mother in her usual practical way.

'Not by father!' I thought.

Afterwards I used to have a special dream about that attic (I had, actually a choice of 3) which I thought about before I fell asleep. There was, in my mind, an old treasure chest up there and when I lifted its creaking lid, I would see mounds of sparkling jewels, all colours of the rainbow. I would plunge my hands into the diamonds, rubies and sapphires which would glint and glimmer as they fell from my hands. Then, smiling, I would sleep.

The days of my childhood always seemed long and interesting with so many things to do, for, like mother, I always liked to be busy.

I never inherited her skill with the needle, but she taught me to hem, to sew blanket stitch and chain stitch. The doll's clothes which I made never fitted very well. Mother must, in retrospect, have saved pounds, and father could not have found a more industrious and frugal lady to marry.

She was even competent in the use of a hammer, nails and a saw and if we needed a cupboard she would produce one out of an orange box. 'I'm not the daughter of a blacksmith for nothing!' she would say and father would sigh as he came home to a cluttered kitchen.

'I'll make your tea in a minute!' mother would mumble, her mouth still full of pins, her sewing machine clattering or perhaps her saw zig-zagging though the side of an orange box.

But a few days later, peace would be restored and the kitchen would resume its normal appearance (although only partially tidy) and meals were presented again on time.

I would usually choose for myself what to do, while the wind sighed outside and the fire kept me warm. Sometimes I decided that my dolls had been neglected for long enough and I would take them out of their cupboard and ask them how they were. I had other things in my cupboard, all my precious possessions books, crayons, little scissors with blunt ends, a sewing set and a little cooker with tiny pans. I once put a Brussels sprout inside a pan, forgot all about it and everybody began to complain about the awful smell.

Father's sister Annie in Scottish costume, who died at the age of 18.

My special treasure was a Weldon's pattern book, with pictures of elegant ladies in the fashion of the day, short knee length skirts and hats which were pulled right down over their eyes. My mother had a hat like that. Sometimes I cut out the dress and coats, leaving little tabs on the shoulders and waist so that I could hook them on to a cardboard figure. Mother had shown me how to do it. I liked using scissors, but I could never understand why I could cut with my right hand and not with my left.

My family of dolls grew as each birthday arrived. Their clothes were all made by mother so that my oldest doll Joan, had a wonderful dress of blue satin. She was my favourite and deserved the best. She had a chubby face with pink cheeks and a pursed up mouth, and eyes which opened and closed heavily, fringed by long lashes. She was called Joan because of me. When I was born, my mother and father had been unable to decide between the names Annie and Joan. It was father who wanted Annie because he had once had a sister of that name. She had 'passed on', they said, at the age of eighteen and father told me that I looked exactly like her. I know this was true because we had a photograph of her dressed in a Scottish costume. She had red hair and blue eyes and could sing like an angel. Red hair was special in my family and father told me that he had been very upset as a boy because the other children at school had laughed at him and declared that he had been left out in the rain so that his hair had gone rusty. I often thought about that other Annie and wondered if, after she had settled in heaven, she could perhaps look down at me. The idea made me feel a bit shivery.

So, to make things right, mother had said 'Call your doll Joan; it's a lovely name'.

She paused, 'And so is Daisy!'

Daisy was mother's own doll and she was made with a white kid body and pottery arms and legs. She was very pale and delicate with pretty fair hair. I looked after Daisy attentively and made sure that she was tucked up in bed if she looked ill.

Then there was Queenie, but there was something about Queenie that I didn't like. She was often naughty and sometimes she told a lie. I knew what lies were and had been told that I mustn't make up stories, which were not true. Queenie had a crack in her head, having once or twice been dropped on the floor. But that was no excuse and I told her quite firmly that I would give her a spanking to teach her a lesson. The strange thing was that she and I were often naughty at the same time, when I myself was slapped on my legs for being a silly girl and a real nuisance. Then I would say to Queenie 'You're a silly doll and a real nuisance!' and I'm afraid that sometimes I used to pull out a tuft of her hair. Course stuff it was, not soft and curly like Joan's. Sometimes I would add, 'If you are naughty again, you'll be sent to bed!'

Years later I was sorry that Queenie had had such a rotten life and when there came the day when I had her no more, I did hope that she had gone to some little child who would treat her better. Probably nowadays, fully repaired and restored, she is sitting in some glass case looking smart and cared for. And I am the only one who knows how she used to be.

Then there was Bosco my dog. I have no idea why he was given that name or who suggested it. He was much loved, so much so that he lost a great deal of his hair and his little stubby tail fell off once or twice and had to be stitched back.

I never had a teddy bear, but there was, at one time, a baby doll, who arrived to complete the family. She had a white silk bonnet edged with swansdown, I loved the swansdown but I never cared much for the baby. It never had a name, which must have meant something. It failed to hold my interest because I couldn't talk sensibly to it. It wouldn't have understood.

I had a lovely cradle too. It was made out of dark wood with a hood and rockers and on the front was carved 'Annie'. Is it like the one Moses had?' I asked.

'Spect so!' replied my grandfather who had made the cradle so very cleverly. He was staying with us at the time.

I loved Granddad, because he had a lovely soft beard which smelled of snuff. He gave me a pinch of it once, and told me not to tell my mother. Sometimes he would come to stay with us for a while and he liked cheese, especially, he said, with maggots crawling out of it.

'That's all reet ' he would say, 'Maggots will only stay in good cheese!' I looked at the cheese, fascinated, and stared as a piece went into granddad's mouth. A bit fell on his beard, but it wasn't a maggot.

His wife was my grandma Martha, whom I don't remember very well, except that she had a quiet calm face and sat silently sewing, like my mother. But she did have two wonderful treasures, a button box and a box of cotton reels in rainbow colours. Dolls were put aside and I spent hours sorting, matching and gloating over all the buttons. Some were made of pearl or glass, some of pink shell, some of fancy metal in a lacy pattern, some of silver and gold. There were five very special ones, which my mother said were made of jet. They were super shiny and carved with patterns and flowers. There were also some nasty ones, which had once been on a thick cloth coat. Big ugly things they were and I thought that they didn't

Grand-dad George, mother's father,
who gave Annie a pinch of snuff!

My mother's family with Grand-dad George and Grandma Martha on the front row.

deserve a place in the button box. Neither did the shirt buttons, work-a-day things, with no attraction.

Both grandma and granddad were with us on the day when Nap arrived, a very large Alsatian with pointed ears. He was welcomed excitedly by my father who thought he would turn out to be a show dog. The trouble was, however, that Nap had a kink in his tail, 'I think that tail might stop him winning' said father thoughtfully. I didn't welcome Nap at first, but because he was handsome and had a good sense of humour, we learned to get along pretty well. Mother insisted that he was too big to stay all the time in the house. There wasn't too much room in the kitchen while he was prancing about, so granddad spent days chopping and hammering old pieces of wood in order that Nap could have a superb kennel in our yard. He had it all to himself and it was big enough for me to walk inside.

But one day, Nap betrayed my trust! He seized Joan! Joan, my very best doll who, fortunately, was not wearing her blue silk dress. He gripped her head between his enormous teeth (I hadn't noticed before how big they were!), and he shook her from side to side. I howled and sat down in a heap, while mother tried to recapture my lovely doll. Father wasn't there to see what his show dog was doing. Joan's eyes blinked in astonishment and rattled ominously as she was thrown about, seized again and dragged under the table. I howled even louder and there was pandemonium, with dog growling and mother shouting.

Finally, Joan was released from the wet jaws of Nap and what I saw made me cry even louder. She had lost her hair! Mother comforted me and said that she would make a little bonnet for her, to match her blue dress.

'It won't show', she said.

'It will! And I will know she has no hair!'

No words could provide any consolation and it was several days before I could gaze with pity and not with horror at poor Joan. Nap was forgiven, because, although he was big, he was still only a puppy and he didn't know any better.

However there was a happy ending. I fervently believed in happy endings because they always happened in my storybooks. That was the way of things when you are happy and only four.

It so happened that mother decided that my hair was too long. It hung down in red curls, right past my ears and down my back, and it always took mother a long time to wash and dry it. I had once seen a picture of Mary Pickford, a poor little girl with dirty hair because she had no mother. She had to have her hair washed in a large tub, with mounds of froth and flying bubbles.

'Mother!' I would say, with my head buried in a wash basin, 'Am I like Mary Pickford now?'

'You are' she would reply, 'But we'll have to cut your hair a bit'.

Sometimes, before I went to bed, she used to help the curls by twisting them in pieces of rag. But now she wanted to cut them off and I didn't want to lose my hair, not one curl. I had grown it and I wanted to keep it.

But when mother was determined, off it had to come! I tried to hide my tears when I saw all the curls, which didn't belong to me any more, lying in a heap on our kitchen floor. But mother tried hard, sometimes! She picked up a handful and said 'We'll keep these in a box, I have a lovely one, just the thing'. So she packed them, one by one, red curls lying close to each other in a box with a frilly paper edge and blue flowers on the lid. And the happy ending? Well one morning after I had my breakfast, mother said 'Here's a parcel for you'.

There was a ribbon wrapped round some paper. It felt, to my eager fingers, like a doll! Wonderful! It was a doll!

I couldn't believe my eyes! There was Joan, a beautiful Joan in a new green velvet dress, shoes to match and gorgeous hair! It curled past her ears and down her back and it looked like mine. It was mine, because mother had stitched it on to a piece of canvas and glued it carefully to her pottery head. I kept her safe and loved her until, like Queenie, I had her no more. Beautiful Joan! I shall never forget her!

When my busy day ended, toys put away and dolls tucked up in their cradle, I was never sorry to climb upstairs to bed. Sometimes a story was read to me, but often I went by myself, after getting undressed by the lovely warm fire. I felt good in my flannelette nightie with roses round the collar and although there was no heating upstairs, somehow I never remember the cold.

My bed was of brass, with knobs on each corner of the bed-stead. Kneeling up, I discovered that I could unscrew a knob to reveal a little secret cavity inside where I could hide a tiny bead or a farthing.

I loved secrets and my inner world which was as real to me as the one I lived in. I would lie in my cosy bed and feel secure, with my feather pillow and thick blankets. Sometimes I would creep out of bed to see if the lamp-lighter was coming. He walked with a lamp and carried along pole with a hook at the end with which he pulled down a chain inside each gas lamp. The light would flicker and flare as it cast its warm glow on the grey pavement, changing the street into a mysterious place.

If I pressed my face to the window I could make a little cloud and if I turned my glance sideways, I could just see the trams on the main road with their sparking trolleys.

A moonlight night of course, was the most magical of all, its silvery gleam resting on the roof tiles and the attic windows.

One night my feet felt cold because I had been standing on the cold lino for ages. I heard mother's voice downstairs. 'I hope you're in bed Annie! And have you said your prayers!'

'Yes' I shouted back and then I realised that, when I did get round to saying my prayers, I would have to confess to telling a lie. I sighed and watched the gas-light with its fan-shaped flame in its little bracket on the wall. Then I remembered that I had not recited my sick list! This was a record, listing all the illnesses I knew. I had already puzzled out, in my four-year-old mind, a kind of philosophy, which worked then and still does! I had great faith in it. Quite simply, if I thought about something threatening then it would not happen! I would have 'magicked' it out of existence where it could not harm me. So, when I heard grown-ups talking about illnesses, I would add the words to my list, even though I could not pronounce them very well. Thus I had listed pneumonia (when people always died after the crises at two in the morning because the world had no more energy), tuberculosis (when people coughed until they died), mumps, boils, bunions and sleepy sickness (when people kept falling asleep). By the time I was considerably older, my list had been lengthened to include an awful skin disease called lupus, which gave me nightmares because I had seen a man with only half a nose Leprosy I hardly dared to think about and I hoped that I would never see a leper. Gall Stones I had also heard about because my uncle had one in a jar, or so he said!

Where did people go when they died, I wondered? I had seen a dreadful picture in father's big family bible, which showed a man called Lazarus coming out of his tomb after he had died. He looked horrid, with bandages wrapped around him and I found all this rather puzzling. The idea of nothingness came back and I began to shout. Mother came up and spoke to me, gently, telling me to think about a garden filled with flowers. So I did. I found a most beautiful landscape, with lavender and marigolds growing in profusion and a little wooden gate. Beyond, were fields of daisies and buttercups, with sheep grazing. A breeze swept over the grass turning it silver. The light faded and I slept.

Chapter 2

Just Five

I WAS NEVER christened. My mother and father said that when I was old enough, I would make up my own mind and sort it out for myself. I didn't quite understand what there was to sort out but I didn't like being different and I envied those children who had been dressed in long white robes, like angel children and had water dripped upon them.

Later, still unsorted, a friend said 'If you aren't christened you won't go to heaven. They won't let you in, so there!' But I disregarded that remark because I had every confidence that, one day I would put everything right with whoever was in charge of the world and who controlled the way into heaven. I knew what the world looked like, with patches of blue and green and the pink bits where our soldiers had marched in and made all the people speak English. But I also knew that kings and queens did not really own the world. It belonged to god and he lived somewhere up in the sky, along with the sun, the moon and the stars. We had to address him politely and say 'Amen' when we had finished. I wondered if he was older than the world and if heaven was different from sky.

I would have liked to ask the star fella who used to come to our house to see my father. He was called Mr. Haffenden and his first name was Alfred. I used to look at him as he sat talking and wondered whether mother was right when she said he never ate bacon, or meat pie, or sausages, but only had fruit juice and vegetables. His wife must have had an easy time because she didn't have to cook anything, but I decided that it wouldn't be very pleasant having to eat raw cabbage and carrots all the time. Maybe onions would be all right because I quite enjoyed their pungent flavour and mother said that when I was a baby I used to sit in my high chair chewing them happily. (But why did they give me onions?)

The star fella never wore a coat, even when it was freezing bitterly in winter, just a jacket over a shirt, and no tie. He said he never felt cold. 'I never think about it!' he said, in his mysterious voice. 'If you think it's cold, then it will be cold. No doubt about that. It's all in the mind, you see!'

I knew then that he wasn't an ordinary man. He was some sort of magician, with a telescope in his home to look at the stars and the stars would tell him things. But where was his long gown and beard?

When we went out I always looked for him and I hoped to catch him dodging out of his house in his long robes covered in moons. But I never did and the star fella stayed disguised as an ordinary man.

I slowly realised that there were things in the world that were not quite what they seemed. People were all different and they didn't all think the same thoughts. Mother said that some people never thought much at all.

Round about this time, my father began complaining about his rheumatism, saying that his knees were stiff and his shoulders ached. Mr. Haffenden sent him to a doctor friend who told him that it would be completely cured if he never ate meat, not one scrap. Mother was very good. Because after that, she gave him cheese and tripe, kippers and rice puddings. Sometimes I saw him eyeing my hot pot and I think he would have liked to have some on his plate instead of those kippers with hundreds of tiny bones. After a year, the pains had gone and we were all very pleased. He still never ate meat.

But one day I had my own problem. In spite of my precautions with the sick list, I got ill.

I was lying in bed and they bought me black custard. I pushed it away, screaming 'I don't want that! It's not real custard!' But they didn't believe me. 'It isn't black' they said, 'Come on! Just a spoonful'.

I had been having the most terrible dreams and my head seemed to be spinning round. Things went very big and then very small and I felt all hot and light, like a balloon. My throat wouldn't allow even a drink to slide down because there was a big lump inside. I had one of fathers' socks wrapped around my neck and they put goose grease on my chest, because it ached.

Sometimes I would sleep and sometimes the gaslights would be there, flickering their fan tails and making evil monsters on the wall. I didn't know where I was. They told me, afterwards, that I'd been covered in spots and that I'd had the Scarlet fever.

But there came a day when I saw my mother's face again and I knew that she'd been there all the time. I was lying in my own brass bed with the little knobs on each corner. There were the familiar patterns on the wallpaper, curling leaves or beautiful birds with long tails. And there, a wonderful sight, was a fire in my bedroom grate, to keep me warm – a real fire with real flames and pieces of coal which fell with a cindery thud.

Sounds were coming from the street and they felt clear cut and new, but far away. My mother felt my forehead.

'Your temperature is down. I think you've getting better. Another week and you'll be as right as rain! I've made you some beef tea, so drink it up. It'll make you strong again.'

I lay in my bed, looking at the fire, with the black poker and a small bucket of coal nearby.

'What day is it?' I asked.

'Monday'.

'Monday's when the coal man comes'.

'He'll be here later. We're ready for another bag.'

Outside, near the cellar window, was a little grid where the coal man tipped the black shiny pieces from his sack. I liked the coal man. He had pink skin streaked with coal dust and a pair of blue smiley eyes and he always said, 'How's the little lass today?' I wondered what his wife said when he came home dirty every day (except Sunday) and how she got his clothes clean. (There was only one man blacker than he was and that was the chimney sweep.) The coal man wore a thick leather jacket with buckles, and gold studs across the back.

'Why does he wear a jacket like that?' I said. 'Is he a knight in armour? Like the one in my story book?'

'He does have a horse!' I added'

'No' replied mother. 'When he heaves a sack of coal from his cart, the studs protect his back. And his cap has a flap at the back to keep out the coal dust.'

'Well his horse thinks he's a knight' I muttered. A little pause. 'When he comes, can I throw down some bread for his horse?'

'You certainly can't. You stay in bed my girl!' I lay back on the pillows and thought of those other horses, which I knew.

They were stabled round the corner, at the back of a very large house with iron gates. They came out into the street every time a dead person had to be taken away in a wooden box.

'What's dead mean?' I said.

'Dead is when you can't speak any more, or open your eyes and your heart stops.'

This was a terrible thing. Now I would always have to make sure that at the end of my sick list, I must say, 'And please! I don't want my heart to stop!'

I admired those horses, as they used to step out with a clattering of hoofs on the cobbles and their coats were the blackest I had ever seen.

'Do they use Nuggett's black shoe polish on their backs?' I asked. 'They're so shiny.'

They wore black feathers on their tossing heads and it was their task to pull a strange cart with glass sides and gold fittings and everyone could plainly see the box inside, with flowers on top. I didn't really like the idea of it, but couldn't help the feelings of expectancy as the horses tossed their heads and turned proudly out of their gate. The traffic stopped, while everybody stood still and the men took off their hats. One of the horses breathed very loudly and in winter its breath made clouds of steam in the cold air. They told me that it had a tube in its throat to help it to breathe and so I called it 'Breather'. Breather and I had a sort of understanding and I'm sure that he felt my sympathy. But one day he had disappeared and they said that his working days were over. He had been sent to the knacker's yard, they told me and I felt sad. I hoped that it was a kind of horsey heaven where the old horse could breathe more easily and where the sun always shone.

I felt better the next day and pleaded to get up out of bed. Mother put my little red dressing gown over my shoulders and I put out one tentative foot. My legs did not feel like mine. To my astonishment they felt weak and wobbly like jelly, as if they had no strong bones inside, I walked slowly round the bed.

'Can I look through the window now? If I walk very carefully?'

Mother fetched a high stool, which granddad had made and I sat down to gaze into Alexandra Grove. It was still very familiar and nothing had changed. Even snowy the cat was there, curled neatly in a windowsill and it occurred to me that if he gave himself a wash he would look more like his name. I was just about to discuss this important topic when I heard, in the distance, a sound which always made me smile,

'Rag Bones! Rag Bones!'

I pressed my nose to the window in order to catch sight of him and tried to shout 'Billy's coming!' But my voice sounded husky and wouldn't come out of my throat properly.

'Rag Bone man!' I croaked.

Then I saw him with his poor bony horse. Progress was slow as he gave people a chance to come out with their rags and other rubbish, (but I never saw any bones). His cart was already piled high with all kinds of jumble, including a set of wheels from a pram. He looked very ragged himself and always wore an old battered hat. I never questioned the economics of the matter, what he did with the rubbish and how he managed to eat and live.

That day Billy had something very special indeed! A bobbing of balloons fastened to his cart! They were bouncing so hard in the wind that I wondered what would happen if they all escaped.

'He's got balloons!' I gasped. 'He'll give you a balloon if you take down some rubbish! See if you can get a red one! Please!'

Mother looked doubtful, 'Well I really need a donkey stone to clean the steps.' A donkey stone was a little square of sandy stone which was rubbed all over the front steps and then washed down with water. All the women of that time cleaned their steps as a matter of pride, (and later it would be my job instead of mother's.)

'You've got some old rags and things, in that sack in the scullery. And you've already got some donkey stones!'

She gave in, went downstairs and I could see her down on the grey pavement holding a red balloon on the end of a string. It was still trying to get away and I did hope that she was holding on tightly. Our sack of rags was thrown into the cart and Billy looked up and waved.

No balloon in my life was ever better than that one!

When father came home from work he was pleased to see me sitting there in a red dressing gown and a balloon to match.

'So the old Scarlet Fever has gone! That's good.'

'Will I get it again?'

'Not likely! But we have to make sure that you're not infectious any more.'

'What's infectious?'

'Well you've had Scarlet Fever germs and we have to make sure that no one else can catch them. So next week we have to have the house fumigated. All this room and all your books and toys will have to be sprayed to kill any germs which may be lurking about.'

A thought struck me!

'Do I have to be fumigated?'

'No', said father. 'Your germs have gone! You're better!'

The following week I was allowed downstairs, and Nap was there to greet me, jumping about and wagging his tail. 'I've had Scarlet Fever, Nap', I told him, 'Have you been a good dog?' He lay down in the rag rug and gazed at me in his doggy fashion.

Everything in the kitchen was the same, but vaguely unfamiliar. There was mother's sewing machine, all closed up with no evidence of its recent use, and the clock was not ticking. But there was the table, set for breakfast. The old and black kettle was making friendly noises on the fire. So it seemed that life had gone on as usual, without me.

The fumigation men came the following day. Mother had pinned up a wet sheet over my bedroom door and upstairs they tramped, carrying a strange looking machine and long pipes. They had a van outside.

I was suddenly worried 'I don't think my dolls will like being fumigated!' I said urgently. 'They won't like getting wet and they won't be able to breathe. So can I bring them down?'

'They have to be done but they won't get wet! You'll see.'

When all was over, they looked just the same, except that they had a very peculiar smell. So life continued happily.

But a few days later, I had another fright. I ran to the bedroom door.

'Mother!' I shrieked. 'I've got Scarlet Fever again! I've got spots!' Mother came in and looked me over.

'That's not Scarlet Fever! You've picked up a flea!'

'I haven't!' I protested. 'I haven't picked up anything!'

'Be quiet!' ordered mother, not too kindly. 'It's an insect which bites. It can jump on you from other people. It's a good jumper is a flea!' She looked at me, 'Maybe you've got it from that cat! It's a dirty old thing!' I squirmed unhappily and began to scratch.

'Don't scratch!' said mother.

'Where is it now? I don't like it!'

Mother rolled back the bedclothes very slowly and carefully, while gazing intently into all the folds and cracks, I stood transfixed.

Then she said triumphantly, 'Here it is! I've got it!' She held up her hand with two fingers clamped together, but I couldn't see anything! Was she joking?

'Is it dead?' I asked

'No, but it soon will be', and she rushed to drown it in a bowl of water.

'Now! We'll put some calamine on those spots and don't scratch! I won't tell you again!'

*   *   *

I once heard a lady say 'That child looks delicate', and I didn't know whether to believe her or not. I had had my share of childhood illnesses but I had every confidence in mother, who always knew exactly what to do. If I had a cold 'n' cough, I was fed on boiled onions, while a little piece of camphor would be hung in a tiny bag around my neck, and under my vest. I also wore a liberty bodice to keep me warm. On Friday nights I had a spoonful of Syrup of Figs, to make me 'go' and in spring I was given some concoction containing Sulphur, to thin my blood and get rid of winter germs. If I fell and scarred my knee, she would use Germolene.

But there were some things I dreaded. I used to cry and heave when I was presented with a mug of mustard and milk to take down my temperature. 'To sweat it out!' said mother firmly. Some of the medicines invented by the doctor were equally nasty and needed a sweet to take the taste away.

'Medicine that tastes bad, does most good!' mother used to say. For a cough I had goose grease rubbed on chest and back and if things got really bad, I had to have a hot poultice slapped upon my chest. Other trusted medicines were 'Fenning's Fever Cure' and 'Parishes Liquid Food' which tasted like cherries.

But father said, one day, that I was having too many sore throats and must be taken to a doctor for a serious talk. We went into a large house and down some steps into an underground room. The floor was covered with black and white checked lino and there was a tiny gas fire at one end, which smelled unpleasant with a flame which continually popped. We sat on uncomfortable chairs and nobody spoke a word, only coughed and sneezed. I decided that the room was full of gas as well as millions of germs, and so I tried to hold my breath.

The doctor called us into the little room. 'Open your mouth!' he commanded.

He pushed down my tongue with something cold and I nearly choked. 'Say Aah!' he said. There was silence for a while, as he peered down my throat, and then he said 'Her tonsils are inflamed, she'll have to have them out!' I was terrified. But father came to my rescue because, when we got home, he said that doctors, clever though they were, might not always be right.

'We'll have a second opinion' he announced to mother. The new doctor had kind eyes, which smiled at me reassuringly through his glasses.

'No,' he said. The tonsils are swollen but they'll be all right. We need our tonsils to trap all the germs.' I began to think that I couldn't cope with all the germs, which seemed to surround me.

The doctor patted me on the head. 'Do as your father tells you.' To my father he said 'Friars Balsam!'

When we got home, I had to put my head under a towel over a bowl of steaming water with Friars Balsam sprinkled in it. I liked the aromatic smell and it felt nice and mysterious under the towel. I imagined all those stupid germs scurrying away from the pungent odour.

'It's good stuff, Friars Balsam! Your throat will soon get better.' And it did. I still have my tonsils.

*   *   *

Mother knew that to keep healthy we had to have good solid food, and so we did, with mounds of potatoes, cabbage and bread 'n butter puddings. There was no balancing of meals or making sure that we had plenty vitamins (which, I think, had not yet been invented!). Eating was always accompanied by 'Eat it all up,' and 'It'll do you good,' or 'Eat those crusts! They'll make your hair curl!'

Sometimes mother used to go to a shop which sold fish and poultry, not my favourite expedition because I hated to see the poor dead fish lying on the marble slab, covered in ice and their mouths wide open. The Fishmonger always had very red hands – he was cold with all that ice. Nor did I like the sight of rabbits, hanging from hooks, with blood on their grey fur and glazed eyes, very dead indeed. Chickens we never had because they cost too much and would have made a large hole in mother's purse. But sometimes she would go to the market at the end of the day, when things were cheap and buy an old hen. This she made father pluck to get rid of the feathers and he also had to take out all the insides. I didn't like the process at all and I suspected that father didn't either, as he sat on a little stool in the scullery, with feathers flying everywhere.

I liked tripe with lots of salt and vinegar but I drew the line at pig's trotter and sheep's head. This was Nap's favourite dinner. There were several things I disliked, including jelly eaten with slices of bread. I hated the crumbs, which got in the way of the slippery jelly and felt that they didn't go together. I still think that I was right. Dislike of prawns came later, but it was all part of the realisation that the feel of food in your mouth was just as important as the taste.

I liked ice-cream too, and sometimes mother would buy some from a man who pushed a strange kind of bicycle with a big blue box in front. She would point to the words on the side which said, 'STOP ME AND BUY ONE'. And sometimes we did.

Talking of food reminds me of the most terrifying occasion of my young life and the most painful. It seems that I had survived Measles, Scarlet Fever and Tonsillitis with all those revolting medicines, lineaments and poultices, with Camphor and with socks around my neck. But now, there was another experience to come. I had never really thought about teeth and though I had been vaguely interested in the things when they fell out without much trouble and I found a fairy penny under my pillow, I believed that I could easily grow some more. But I didn't understand that sometimes they went bad and began to ache. One such tooth did not fall out and I started to realise that it never would. Mother held warm cloths against my throbbing cheek and I cried. My father began to talk to mother about someone called a 'Dentist'.

After a day or so, the tooth ached less and I began to think that I'd won another battle. But no! I was taken to see the Dentist, a Mr. Smith who lived round the corner of Alexandra Grove and he was going to pull out my bad tooth.

'I don't want to go!' I howled, 'It's better!'

'No it isn't. It might ache again and you wouldn't like that, now would you? He won't hurt you.' But this was a lie, as I later found out, and I felt very disappointed with my mother.

The dentist's room was dark, with a very bright light over a leather chair. There was a little basin and a glass with pink water. They sat me down in the chair and I felt weak with terror and it was the first time that I heard anyone say, 'Open your mouth wide!' (But not the last), and the dentist had some trouble making me do it. He held his fingers inside my mouth and spoke, over my head, to mother.

He said, 'I can't give her anything because she'll never open her mouth again!' Quite right! I wouldn't have! I saw something bright and shiny in his hand and something had changed on my teeth. There was an awful crunching and an agonising pain shot my nose, up into my head and out at the top.

'There we are!' said Mr. Smith. 'It's out! Look!' He held up my tooth covered in blood and I cried bitterly. But after rinsing my mouth with pink water and spitting it out, I felt better and stopped crying. Mother wrapped my face and head in a warm woolly scarf and gave me a handkerchief to put over my mouth so that the hole in my gum wouldn't catch cold. The dentist gave me the tooth to keep.

'That's a shilling please,' I heard Mr. Smith say. It wasn't the last time that I saw him and he must have earned a hoard of shillings by pulling out people's teeth, because, later on, he moved to a finer home with a waiting room where people sat in petrified silence, pretending to read magazines.

All this of course, made me very aware that bodies could sometimes go wrong and that there were all manner of nasty things waiting to pounce. That is why my sick list was so important – a kind of insurance against getting ill.

So obsessed did I become that, at the age of ten, I wrote a play with dialogue between Mr. Kidney, Mr. Liver, Mrs. Blood and General Heart. And even later, a friend helped me to write the first edition of Skeleton Pictorial, (although no others actually followed!).

But I also decided that god must be a wonderful person to make human beings who grew from baby-size into tall people.

Chapter 3

Going up to Six

THE DAY CAME when I had to go to school. I had turned five in March and my new life was scheduled to begin the following September. I thought of it with a mixture of excitement and trepidation. I knew where the school was because mother had often taken me past it 'To get used to the idea,' she said to father.

I had peered through the stiff black railings, pointed like spears, at the enormous grey playground and the alarmingly large red building, which was the school. I had gazed with some disquiet at the boys and girls, all shapes and sizes, whizzing about in the playground, with their flying arms and countless legs. And I didn't know any of them.

There was also the question of boys who had not, at the time, figured large in my short life. I thought they looked very rough, with dirty boots, holey jerseys and loud shrill voices.

Granddad was staying with us at the time and he smiled at me through his soft white beard, his eyes all crinkly round the edges. 'Them's laughter lines,' he would say. Mother looked over at me 'Granddad's going to take you to school and bring you back for dinner.' She said no more.

So the next day, at the end of summer, when all the playing stopped and the children were sent back to school, I took hold of granddad's hand, ready as ever I would be, for my new adventure. I said goodbye to mother, to my dolls and to Nap our dog. Mother had made look pretty because I have a photograph of my class and there I am, on the back row, with a large white bow like a butterfly. No-one else had a bow like that and I felt very proud. It also reminded me of mother and knew she was not too far away.

There were fifty boys and girls. Some looked very young like me, but a few looked so unconcerned and worldly-wise that they appeared old already. But none looked very happy and one small girl was apt to go off and cry in a corner. The boys looked a burly lot but gave me no trouble and a girl called Sylvia let me sit on a little chair next to her.

I got used to it after a while, as the strange new world of school gradually grew more familiar. Every morning we would leave our little

Annie in her Fives class with large white bow.

tables and chairs and trot off into a big hall where would say our prayers and sing my favourite hymn.

'Jesus bids us shine with a clear pure light,
Like a little candle, shining in the night.
In this world of darkness, so we must shine,
You in your small corner and I in mine.'

Then we each had a straw mat to sit on (Oval – shaped), and we were given a small piece of paper and a tin of wax crayons. There was also a piece of Plasticine and I can remember the smell of it.

I could already read the easy books and soon got bored. I also knew all the numbers, which were pinned like large dominoes, round the classroom walls. I was very surprised to learn that some of the children could not even count, let alone recognise the numbers and wondered why their parents hadn't helped. I watched them trying hard, with much sucking of thumbs and a twisting of one foot around the other.

I don't remember what I learned but I did find out one important thing. I could draw! One of my drawings was pinned up on the wall and one day, when all the mothers and fathers were invited into school, there it was, for all to see.

'That's very good Annie!' said a smiling Miss. She turned to father, 'See! She's got a path going smaller as it goes into the distance!' Above the smiles and appreciative noises, I gazed at it with renewed interest. It looked just as I knew it should look and I had not found it difficult to do.

It was the last time granddad came to visit for, soon afterwards, his heart became very tired and he died. I loved him and felt that I had lost something in my life which, was very important. After that, my mother used to take me to school, across the busy main road and as far as the school gates and the iron railings. When school finished, she was always there, along with the other mothers and the babies in prams.

I got used to going and to the daily routine of school which, never changed, and because it didn't, I felt secure and quite contented. The children stayed the same too; the teachers never left and must have remained there all their lives. There was a head mistress, kindly but not so often seen. Sometimes stern looking men came to look at us, to see if we were being good and learning our lessons well. And occasionally the nit nurse came! We all had to stand in line while the nurse, not too gently, examined our hair to see if we had nits. 'They're catching,' teacher explained, 'and have to be got rid of before they turn into lice.' It sounded quite frightening but happily I was never discovered to have any of the horrid creatures.

Then one day, I had a new friend called Mabel. She had a pig- tail and she lived near us in Plymouth Grove. She went to my school too, but, because she was older than me, she had to go upstairs to the senior department. Mother arranged for her to take me to school, so every day she called at our house, took me by the hand across the main road and round the corner to school where, as if it were suddenly important to get there early, we began to run. Through the gates, across the playground we went, pell-mell and then I watched Mabel, pig-tail flying, as she clattered up the worn steps to the mysterious region where the big children spent their day.

'I'm ink monitress today!' she panted, 'Ta Ta for now!' Mabel didn't like school at all and often said so.

'I can't wait till I'm fourteen,' she used to say, 'Then I can leave school! I don't know why we have to wait that long!'

She paused for thought, 'It's because the grown-ups don't know what to do with us, I suppose. School keeps us out of trouble!'

She lived in an enormous house, which used to be very grand but which was now deserted, except for Mabel's family, who lived in three rooms at the back.

Two broken pillars held up a porch over the front door which was no longer used. Walls were cracked and blackened, and I lost count of all the windows. She had a mother and father and two brothers. It didn't cost any money to live there, she said, because her father looked after all the wagons and horses which, were kept in stables. Later, the horses went and were replaced by steam engines which pulled the large wagons – noisy dirty things which had to have coal shovelled in to heat up the boilers.

I didn't like Mabel's father and found him frightening. He was a huge man, always black with coal dust, and only a bit of white showing round his eyes. He had bushy, overhanging eye-brows and a prickly chin. His clothes were always dirty and I used to call him the 'Black Man'. When he came in for his tea and I was in the kitchen, I would hide behind Mabel. I never remember him saying one word when her mother put down his plate of food on the table and he ate it very noisily with his mouth open. 'Why doesn't he say thank you?' I said to Mabel. She just shrugged.

Sometimes, on a Saturday, I used to go there for my tea. Her father had washed off all the coal dust, put on a clean shirt and had gone to the pub in the town. So I felt safe. We always had the same tea, a very small piece of ham, a pickled onion from a jar and a slice of bread, followed by a plate of jelly. Mabel's mother was not pretty and she always looked sad and weary because she had so much work to do. She had once been a young servant girl in a posh house belonging to rich people, until along came Mabel's father who (as Mabel put it), 'Swept her off her feet.' That sounded very rough to me and I think it had something to do with the fact that she always stood on one leg. She had painful sores which, were always bandaged up and wouldn't heal. It isn't easy to balance on one leg. I knew, because I had tried it and I used to feel really sorry that she had to stand like that. Once, Mabel came to our house crying because her father had kicked her mother's leg.

'He did it on purpose!' she sobbed. 'I'd like to kick him! Or hit him on the head with a chair! I will one day.'

After tea, we always went to the bathroom, reaching it along a dark creepy corridor with one high up gas light. Then up a twisting flight of steps, I would never have dared to go on my own.

But the bathroom was wonderful! It had a large toilet seat made of wood, and a chain with a white pottery handle which said 'PULL'. There was also a large bath which, someone had once tried to paint but it was all chipping off. Mabel told me that the water used to come out of the ceiling.

'Does it come out now?' I asked.

'No. Stopped working long ago. Look up there! You can see all the holes.'

'But why!' I asked, 'Water should come out of the tap.'

'Well rich people used to live here, with lots of servants and it was very posh to have a bath with water coming out of the ceiling!'

'Oh,' I said, 'What a funny thing!'

In the kitchen were rows of bells with curly springs, high up on the wall. In the old days, a bell used to ring when the lady of the house wanted a maid. We used to make up names for the servants and imagined that each one had a bell of her own.

'That one is Mary's,' I said.

'And that one's for Edith!' said Mabel'

'And that one's for Mrs. Scrub – the – Floor.'

'That's not a name!'

'Tis.' And we fell about laughing

The kitchen was so big that Mabel's mother must have walked miles each day, just to build up the fire, fill the kettle and cook the meals. I was always glad to be taken home, for our tiny kitchen, with mother in it, always felt safe and bright.

*   *   *

One day, a Sunday I think it was, we were invited out to another big house. Aunt Lizzie Brown, who was my father's cousin, lived there 'In solitary splendour' as he used to say. I was wearing my best dress and coat, (made by mother), and I trotted along, sedately.

But after a while it became too much effort and I began to dawdle.

'Pick up your feet!'. Mother sounded quite cross. She was always saying that.

'You'll scuff your shoes and wear out the shoe leather.' Wearing out the shoe leather was one of mothers worries, I suppose.

Do you like going to Aunt Lizzies?' I asked, guessing correctly that it was merely one of her duties.

'Sometimes', she said.

'Why doesn't father come to see his cousin?'

'Too busy. Besides it's a lady's job.'

Four steps led up to Aunt Lizzie's front door and we could hear the bell ringing deep inside the house. Suddenly, there she was, staring down at us from her top step and I thought she was a giantess. When I had climbed the steps she resumed a normal proportion except that she was rather fat, with two chins. Her dress was black with silver beads on the front and her eyes were steely like the beads. So was her voice.

'Come in!' she commanded and I realised at once that here was a lady who must be obeyed.

'Quick sharp!. Wipe your feet child! Don't dirty the carpet!'

Held in unblinking gaze, I carefully wiped one foot and then the other.

A long hall disappeared into the back of the house and on the left was a parlour, with a huge window smothered darkly in lace and dark brown velvet curtains. A large leafy aspidistra in a fancy pot, kept out even more light.

There were ornaments everywhere and gloomy pictures on the walls, of stags and ships at sea. I had never seen such large furniture. The sideboard would never fit into our front room, that was certain, not to mention all the cabinets and cupboards, the stiff chairs and the tiny tables. I couldn't keep my eyes off the sideboard with its lion's feet. There were lion's heads carved on the doors and an array of fancy bottles and a large mirror set in dark wood. A tiny fire was burning in the grate and it gave out a great deal of smoke.

I thought it remarkable that everything was larger than life, including Aunt Lizzie herself, but not the tiny fire which was struggling to burn at all. She gave it a poke, which made it worse, muttering that coal was very expensive.

'Well sit down!' she commanded. 'Annie! You may sit on that little chair'

It had a prickly seat which hurt my legs and I was compelled to sit there, wriggling.

'Sit still', said mother, not understanding at all. Then she and Aunt Lizzie began to talk, as grown-ups do, about the weather, about father and the family. I didn't know all the names, so I stopped listening. A large clock with a round face, like the moon, was ticking on the mantlepiece and I thought that it was the only cheerful thing in the room. Next to it were some pottery figures, some photographs in frames and a splendid pair of red glass vases, hung with pieces of crystal. I wanted to touch them and to make them tinkle, but I couldn't reach them (which was just as well).

Another few wriggles on the prickly chair and then I began to wonder if Aunt Lizzie would notice if I went a little walk round that fascinating room. Because her back was tuned to me, she never noticed as I silently slid off the chair and tip-toed to a cupboard crammed with flowery tea-sets, with teapots to match. She must be very rich, I thought, especially as she was wearing four gold rings with coloured stones and a very large glittery broach. Why had my father never mentioned that he had such a wealthy lady as his cousin? I wondered where she kept all her money and whether she had a secret hiding place for it all.

Then my eye fell upon a large mysterious box decorated with birds and flowers. Was this where she kept it? Would it be full of silver coins? Just at that moment, as I was going to lift the lid, my mother turned and saw me. I gave a jump.

'Annie!' exclaimed mother. 'Don't ever do that again! You were told to sit on that chair, so that's where you should be!'

'But it's prickly!' I said.

Aunt Lizzie's mouth was pressed into a thin line and her beads flashed ominously.

'That child needs taking in hand!' she said and swept out to fetch in the tea. What a strange thing to say, I thought. I was far too big to be picked up in someone's hand. Then tears came to my eyes as mother scolded me yet again for poking into things that didn't belong to me.

'But I only wanted to see if there were any gold and silver and diamonds! Do you know what's in the box?'

'Layo'ers for meddlers!' retorted mother, which she always said if I got too curious. My father was kinder because he called me Miss Curiosity, which sounded better than being called a meddler.

I was on my chair again, looking wistfully round and wishing it was time to go home.

'Will Aunt Lizzie bring a piece of cake?'

'Not very likely. Not after that performance'

She was right. No cake. Just a few plain biscuits which looked like those we gave to Nap. One biscuit fell onto the carpet and on trying to pick it up, I trod on the thing, making an awful crumby mess. Aunt Lizzie snorted like a pig and, with an angry clatter, she reached for a little brass shovel and brush in the fireplace. The crumbs flew about angrily before settling in the shovel. I squirmed again in my seat. Aunt Lizzie glared at me, then shook her head so that her chin wobbled.

'Doesn't that child ever sit still?' She said to mother.

'Well,' mother started to reply.

'Now look here!' Lizzie interrupted. 'If she can sit on this little stool for ten minutes, then I'll give her a threepenny bit!' She was probably quite despairing. But a threepenny bit! Had she made a mistake? Well, if she had, she couldn't change it now and I was resolved to have that threepenny bit if I had to sit there all day!

So I settled down meekly on the little stool and it was very hard. I gazed at a picture of the deer with long antlers which hung over the fireplace and, like the Hurdy Gurdy Monkey, it had a pair of very sad eyes. I counted the bobbles on a table cloth. I yawned. How long was ten minutes? I tried to think about things, and then I tried not to think at all. I looked at the ticking clock and wished I could tell the time.

But the ten minutes did pass and there came the happy moment when mother said.

'Well thank you for the tea Lizzie! It's time we went home'

So I got my threepenny bit and I held it tightly in one hand until mother said I'd lose it and she would put it in her purse.

'Is Aunt Lizzie very rich?' I asked. 'Does she really keep her money in a secret place?'

Mother hurried on, talking as she went.

'Well not very rich but not without a few pennies either! She used to work for a Greek lady who died and left her all the beautiful things you saw. I don't know where she keeps all her money, but I know something! She won't spend two pence where a penny will do! You were lucky to get a threepenny bit, I can tell you'

At five and a half years old, if I could have made a list, I would have realised that I knew quite a number of people, all different and all doing different things. Some of them I liked, but some, like Aunt Lizzie and the Black Man, I didn't care for at all. The people I disliked were always large with cold eyes and I learned that if you looked at people's eyes, you would know what they were like inside.

There was, for instance, Mr. Dromgoole. He had mean little piggy eyes and he didn't mean what he said. I knew that.

Now and then he used to come to see father to look at those large books and all the inky numbers on the pages with lines ruled across. I felt that his visit was not very necessary and that father could get his sums right, without any help from him. Before he came, father would have to work extra hard at 'doing his books'. Too hard, I thought and it was Mr. Dromgoole's fault, the mysterious Mr. Dromgoole who came and went like a ghost.

He lived somewhere far away and had to come on a tram. He was always dressed in a dark grey suit with a bowler hat, a briefcase in his hand, and a rolled-up umbrella with a curly handle in case it rained.

Today he would be coming for his tea and he would be there when I arrived home from school. So, when Mabel had deposited me at the top of our street, my footsteps slowed down. It had just begun to rain and I looked at the spaced-out spots appearing on the pavement. I had left my raincoat at school and my mother would be cross. Then, a little way ahead of me I saw Mr. Dromgoole just turning into our house. There was the bowler hat, the umbrella opened because of the rain, a grey raincoat and neatly polished shoes. I slowed down and took my time in arriving at Number Nine. I decided to go into the house by the back door, past Nap's kennel. Nap was inside being a good dog, but when he heard me, he came out and wagged a greeting.

As I passed the kitchen window, I could see Mr. Dromgoole sitting at our kitchen table, waiting for his tea. He had a boiled egg on a plate in front of him and I caught a glimpse of his plump hand, with a spoon, ready to slice off the top. I opened the back door and went in.

'Where's your mac Annie?' said mother, noticing at once that I wasn't wearing it.

'Left it at school have you? A lot of use that is, when it's raining!'

Mr. Dromgoole looked at me, his small eyes almost disappearing in the folds of his fat cheeks.

'How nice to see you Annie', he said politely, and he didn't mean it, I knew.

Mother said, 'Wash your hands and come and have your boiled egg.'

When I sat down, I saw at once that Mr. Dromgoole had the brown egg which was saved for me.

'I've got a white egg!' I exclaimed in disgust.

'White! Brown! What's the difference! Eat it up!'

I was really upset, because of course brown eggs tasted better than the white ones! I watched the movement of Mr. Dromgoole' jaws as he chased food from one bulging cheek to the other. Then I noticed that mother didn't have an egg, only bread and butter. His fault, I thought. He's eating my mother's boiled egg.

'And how is Annie today ?' he said. 'Got all your sums right like your father. I never find anything wrong with your father's sums either!' He gave a kind of crumby laugh, which was the best he could do.

Then why, I thought did he have to come? I decided to ask.

'Why do you look at my father's sums?' I said.

'I'm an auditor, that's why. It's my job to check if they're correct. As I said, they always are.'

After tea, they went, Mr.Dromgoole and father, into the little middle room with the roll-top desk. Father had ready the big brown books, with gold lettering on the front. Inside the books were rows and rows of neat blue figures, marching up and down and some red lines which they hadn't to cross. Nearby was a metal box with a key and a label on top which said 'Contributions'.

'What contributions?' I had once asked mother.

'Well- your father collects Insurance money from people, and sick money for when they are ill. So he has to write down what they pay in a ledger book.'

'So that he won't forget. I see.', I said in my most solemn voice, to show that I understood.

That's what they were doing – inspecting numbers and counting money. They hadn't finished when I went to bed, but soon afterwards, I heard Mr. Dromgoole's voice, as he went off to catch his tram.

'All signed and correct' he said in a booming voice, as if he was glad it was all over. 'A pleasure to see you again, I'm sure.'

The next morning, father showed me the name. H. A. Dromgoole. Auditor. March 1926. I breathed a sigh of relief. No more of the horrid Mr. Dromgoole for a while!

Annie aged four, with mother and father.

Chapter 4

No Sisters or Brothers but Plenty of Cousins

UNT JENETTE was the reason why, quite suddenly, my life changed. She was another cousin of my Father's, so was not really my Aunt. She lived thirty miles away in what had been, in my parents' day, little more than a village, but which was now growing into a small industrial town centred round the Motor Works and the cotton mills.

When her letter came, she was quite unknown to me and I had no recollection of who she was. Apparently, she was very old and in need of care, so she wrote to ask if we would leave our house in Alexandra Grove and go to live in hers. It meant that my poor Mother would become her housekeeper, cook and nurse, all rolled into one.

'What do you think?' asked Father. 'It'll save the rent'.

As so often occurs when remembering a childhood event, there is the dream-like situation where you are happily settled in one particular place and then you find yourself in another, with no real knowledge of how you got there.

However, we all arrived at Number Two Thurston Road, when I was exactly six and we stayed until I was eight. Nap, the Alsation went with us too, travelling in the Guard's van on the train. He had a kind of kennel made in a shed in the small back-yard. My Father had to travel, every weekday, to his work in Manchester, using the train and then a tram. He told me that he used to pass Alexandra Grove and I felt sad when he mentioned it because I missed the Milkman, the Coal-man and Billy with his bony horse.

Aunt Jenette's house was the first one of a long terrace and had a privet hedge at the front. I remember that hedge very well for I once found a number of intriguing pieces of gold tissue paper.

They were blowing about in the street and as they did not appear to belong to anyone, I was allowed to keep them.

'They're gold leaf', said my Mother.

I experimented happily by rubbing off the gold and I turned a whole pile of privet leaves into a treasury of magical gold which didn't adhere

very well but pleased me greatly.

Aunt Jenette's house was furnished with dark old pieces of furniture and smelled musty because the windows had been kept closed. But I did have my own tiny bedroom, with a window overlooking the road. A box-room they said it was and it certainly felt like that. Right opposite was a large building which stretched from one end of the street to the other. There were hundreds of windows and I occasionally caught a glimpse of some of the people working inside, like bees in a hive. It was part of the Motor Works, rapidly growing and taking over the little town. At twelve o'clock, on the dot, a siren would wail as if a monster ruled and had to be obeyed. Suddenly the doors would open and out poured hundreds of people with loudly pattering feet, all anxiously running. Across the main street, another Works was spilling out its slaves, many of them wearing clogs so that the whole world seemed full of clatter. (At the bottom of each clog was an iron horse-shoe which could make sparks and sometimes had to be repaired at the cloggers).

I soon found out where everyone was going and why! It had been a long time since breakfast and they were all hungry! Some of them poured into the pie shop, or the chip-shop while some jostled round a Cart to buy hot peas. Others sat on low walls to eat their butties, very thick ones known as Tram-stoppers. Half an hour later, they would trickle back into the buildings, slowly this time, without urgency. (Who wants to rush back to work?)

It was in that little bedroom where I had Chicken Pox and so I had to miss a very important happening, which, they told me, was a total eclipse of the sun, when the light would be blotted out by the moon, the world would go dark and the birds would stop singing. People were planning to go out with pieces of smoked glass to look through so that the sun, before it slid away, would not hurt their eyes.

'Will it come light again?' I asked anxiously.

'It's dark for a few minutes that's all. The moon will move away and the sun will come out again. It's best to look at it from the top of a hill'.

I begged and pleaded to go, but no, I was not given permission to leave my room. I remained there, tearful and heart-broken, with my bedclothes over my eyes and I saw nothing. It was some time before I could forgive the doctor and my parents for denying me such a wonderful spectacle, especially as they said it wouldn't happen again until I was a very old lady.

Then another dreadful thing occurred. One day my Father told me that Aunt Jenette didn't like Nap and so he had to go. She didn't want him living in the back yard, she said. Tears were not far away. I had, long ago, forgiven Nap for tearing off Joan's hair and I wanted him to be happy.

'Where will he go?' I whispered sadly. Father told me that Mr.

Tomlinson, a man who owned a newsagents shop across the road, would take him in and would look after him very well, because he was an expert on dogs. I wondered if Nap would like living in a shop, among all the newspapers and magazines and I thought that it was a good thing that he had given up tearing things to pieces. Anyway he settled happily with Mr. Tomlinson (and I still used to see him occasionally). He managed to straighten out the kink in his tail so that he did become a Show Dog and he even won a prize and a large rosette to wear on his collar. I was very proud of that dog and showed everyone his picture in the paper, where he was smiling happily with a beautiful straight tail.

Aunt Jenette reminded me of Aunt Lizzie and I wondered if Father had any other strange cousins. (Well yes! He had! But I came to know that, much later).

Like Cousin Lizzie she didn't like children either, and any noise would send her into a temper, so that the house had to remain very quiet indeed. She was a small lady, who looked as if she had once been taller but had shrunk with the passing years. She was extremely thin with bony hands on which you could see the purple veins and her stern face was made even more severe by the gold glasses which pinched her nose. I never once saw her smile, so there was no laughter in Two Thurston Road and I missed it, because I thought that smiles, giggles and hearty laughs were attractive things to hear. My Mother said that she was indeed a sour-apple kind of lady and you could tell that this was so. Besides, she had a mouth like a trap.

'Ready for snapping at people' I said rather cleverly. But is seemed worth trying not to upset her and to simply do what she asked.

'I don't think she's very happy' I remarked.

'People like that never are '.

I wondered how it was that lovely pink chuckling babies could turn into such crotchety people as cousins Jenette and Lizzie.

From that time on, if I was ever 'in a mood' my Mother would say, with frightening conviction, 'Yes and if you go on like that, young lady, you'll be like Aunt Jenette before you're much older!'

This was horrifying and I would make an effort to turn my mouth up instead of down and not to be a crosspatch any more. I certainly didn't want a mouth which stayed stiff and unbending as a ruler, nor did I want all those lines caused by a perpetual frown.

One day, when we were alone, Mother told me more about Aunt Jenette, how she was called Mrs. Lewis. I think Mother had to talk to someone because, like me, she was frustrated at having to tip-toe about the house, making sure that she didn't rattle the pots or the fire-irons.

'Is there a Mr. Lewis?' I had queried.

Mother was sewing and her needle was flashing in and out.

'No. He's dead years ago. He was a Welshman from Wales. She didn't have a husband for a long time. She was a maiden lady. Then she answered that advertisement in the paper'.

I knew what an advertisement was.

'What did it say?'

'I don't know. Well maybe it said 'Wanted. A kind lady to be a dutiful wife''.

'But she wasn't kind!' I said. Mother ignored that.

'Anyway, they met at a station and he had told her to look out for a man with a red carnation in his coat buttonhole'.

I was fascinated at the thought of Aunt Jenette sitting, bolt upright and unsmiling on a platform bench, watching the train steam in and then stop with a clanging of doors. There he would be, smart in his best suit with a waistcoat and a watch-chain, a red carnation in his lapel. Did she, I wondered, feel excited, or nervous! I found it hard to imagine her being any younger or having worn anything more attractive than her usual sombre dress.

'I wonder if she liked him?' I reflected.

'Liking didn't come into it! He was, I believe, quite a handsome man. Had been married before, so I expect he was lonely. Anyway, they must have hit it off, because Aunt Jenette became Mrs. Lewis and they came to live in this house'.

A thought suddenly struck me.

'You didn't have to advertise for my father, did you mother?'

'I certainly did not! I wouldn't do such a thing! A man should look around and find a nice lady for himself and she should wait until she's found!'

I understood. A lady must do nothing – just sit in her house, and wait until a man passed by and looked through her window, or perhaps he would be in Church saying his prayers next to her in the pew or maybe he would help her if the wind blew away her hat. She must be sedate and quiet and not look him in the eye.

As time went on, Aunt Jenette used to stay in her bed for a long time and sometimes, she never came downstairs at all. Poor Mother did all the running up and down in between doing the housework and all the washing. She was always washing sheets. This was while Father was at work.

Then came the day when my cousin Bessie took me to school which was a bit frightening because once there, we were in different classes. But it didn't take long to get used to a new routine. It was a Wesleyan Chapel School where my parents went when they were of school age. It stood next to the large old chapel where they were married and where Mother used to sing in the choir.

There was a large hall, divided up into various classes, with a high platform at one end. I remember singing 'Summer suns are glowing, over land and sea' and to me it was always summer time. I cannot remember the winter at all (except Christmas time). The other children were nice enough and all perfectly obedient, except for a few with runny noses and one little lad who had all his hair shaved off.

'Why?' I whispered to Bessie as we passed him on our way home.

'He's got Ringworm!' she said.

I didn't really want to look, but I couldn't resist giving a quick glance.

Sure enough, there were some round pink patches on his head, but I couldn't see any worms.

'Can't see any worms' I said.

But it sounded very serious and I put Ringworm on my Sick List, so that I wouldn't get it. Another child had bent legs. Bandy legs we called them and they used to say, rather cruelly, 'Well, he couldn't stop a pig in an alley!'

The nit-nurse used to call, just as she did at my other school. One little girl looked very poor with holes in her socks and she lived in a street where people had problems. She had to have her hair washed in Carbolic soap because the nurse found nits.

'You can catch nits, like fleas', I said to Bessie.

'I know', she replied.

Mother said, when I told her, that it was best not to sit too near, so the poor little girl had no friends except for another child, who also had nits, so it didn't really matter.

It was at this school in the playground, that I met my first sweetheart. I played my part beautifully being dutifully quiet and keeping my eyes down, like Mother had said. Then, at one corner of the playground, away from the others, he gave me a ring out of a penny lucky bag. So it was a very shy affair and his name was Fred. I told Bessie about him and said, 'You're not to tell'. She never did. Until later!

Bessie and I were good friends. She lived with her parents, her two older brothers and a sister in the house which adjoined the Smithy where, until a short time ago, our Granddad had been the Blacksmith. My parents bought me a wooden scooter so that I could go on my own to the Smithy house, and I went often, in perfect safety, taking short cuts along the back streets. Mother used to grumble because I always wore out my left shoe which was the one that did the scooting. I tried to change over my feet and scoot the other way round, with the right one doing all the work, but I never could. Once or twice I fell off and hurt my knee. I got black grit in it and Mother put iodine on it to stop it from going septic. But it healed and skinned over the grit which never came out.

We used to play at shop, Bessie and me, borrowing things from the real Smithy Shop, like nails and screws, baking tins, curtain rings and tin tacks. There was a very fat lady who used to live across the street in a house with a flight of steps and an iron railing leading up to the front door. We used to shout Pelly Norter across the street when no one in Bessie's family could hear us. Her real name was Nellie Porter!

Bessie's mother was a very kind lady who used to walk very slowly, as if she was in a procession. Now and again she would give a heavy sigh. I wondered if she felt tired, with four children to look after and all the meals she had to cook. At dinner time the family would sit rather noisily round a large wooden table and I was a quiet little mouse jammed in amongst them. My favourite meal was Toad-in-the hole made with sausages, but I could never manage to finish my helping, although my cousins used to polish off huge mounds of food. I was gently chided.

'You won't grow if you don't eat!', so I used to try to swallow it all. But I could never swallow the skin on a rice pudding. Just as well, for my cousins really clamoured for it and quarrels arose if two people claimed that it was their turn.

'Bags the skin!' They would shout, but I said nothing.

My two cousins used to play with us in the dirt yard at the back of the Smithy. The eldest, called George, was rather rough.

'He doesn't realise his own strength', they said and I soon discovered the truth of this, as he whirled me round and knocked me down. I ended up with a scar on my chin which only faded with the years. Once he fell off a swing and broke his leg.

One day I was sent to Bessie's house to be out of the way, because Aunt Jennet was very ill. There was a very strange smell about the house, mingling with disinfectant. My Mother was going up and down the stairs and into the bedroom where the door was always firmly shut behind her. A week later, Aunt Jennette had died and I was allowed to return.

'What happened to her?' I wanted to know.

'I told you. She died!'

'Yes, but what did you do?'

'The Doctor came. And then Mrs. Butler came to lay her out'.

'Lay her out?'

'Yes – well. She made her look nice with a clean nightie'.

'Did she go in a coffin?'

'Yes of course. And now she's buried in the grave-yard, near to the big Church. We'll go tomorrow and take her some flowers'.

So we went to where the Norman Church stood solid and proud, with its square tower reaching up towards the sky. A low grey wall surrounded the countless graves, which, before my astonished eyes, lay row by row and line by line.

'What a lot of dead people!' I said, 'And they've nearly all got flowers. So how will you find Aunt Jenette?'

But we found her easily. She was lying in a freshly dug grave covered by black soil, near to some lovely beech trees where the wind only whispered and leaves fell silently.

'She won't be cross now, will she?' I observed.

Mother shook her head and put her flowers into a jam jar. A wreath of flowers was already there.

'Will she know that you have given her those?' I said.

'I hope she will', replied Mother.

Then she took me to see Granddad's grave, the lovely man with the beard which smelled of snuff. He was sharing his grave with Grandma Martha and I was glad that he wasn't lonely. Two children were running in and out of the graves and I felt that it was wrong because dead people would not like the sound of pounding feet.

From then on, whenever we visited the graveyard, it became a source of great fascination. I found that some little children were lying there, young ones who had gone to heaven at a very early age. On one stone was carved 'Here lies Mary Trelfall, aged 3, who went to Jesus on April 4 1914. May she rest in peace'.

I also found a Monkey's grave and one which showed carvings of an axe and chopping block. I pulled at Mother's arm. 'Look there', I said. 'Someone must have had his head chopped off!' said mother. 'Or maybe it belongs to the man who did the chopping!'

I was filled with horror, 'Why did he lose his head?' I whispered.

'Because he had done something very wrong'. I worried for days, wondering what wrong a person had to do in order to have his head chopped off.

'Do they chop off heads now?' I hardly dared to ask.

'No, of course not!' replied Mother

'That's all right then!'

But nobody told me at the time that they were hanged instead.

On the way out, I tried not to walk on the flat grave-stones of dead people which lay like paving stones around the Church itself. Perhaps they had been poor, I thought, unlike those who had grave-stones like large tables, or with splendid black marble affairs with their names in gold letters.

Certainly not like the ones with beautiful stone angels, with their wings outstretched, guarding children like little James or little Adam who had died before life had scarcely begun.

I held Mother's hand because somehow I needed to. As I turned to look back and though I did not fully understand, I felt the peace, the mystery and some strange link with the soil. Wherever I smell rotting leaves or damp earth, I always remember.

*   *   *

Although Father had several cousins whom I met and knew, I also had nineteen cousins of my own, as well as nine uncles or aunts. Perhaps this compensated for being the only one in my own family, but I always wished that I had a brother or a sister. Some of my cousins were near in age to myself and those I knew best. While living at Aunt Jenette's I saw them often and later, when we returned to Manchester, we used to go back and visit them, all in their separate houses. Three of them lived in shops. Two were ironmonger's and one was a baker.

On the whole, my cousins were a jolly lot and we had good times, especially at Christmas. Apart from Bessie and her brothers and sisters, there was a pair of twins in the family. I could never tell one from the other, but they always twinkled at me with their eyes and never seemed to mind. I often thought what fun it would be for one to pretend to be the other and wonder if they ever did. Their Father, Uncle Eb, had once lived in Australia and had brought back some ostrich eggs – large smooth ovals, placed on wooden stands on top of a high chest-of-drawers. I could just reach and, with my insatiable curiosity, of course, I just <u>had</u> to stand on tip-toes and touch. To my utter horror, one went crashing to the floor, shattering in too many pieces to mend. I was petrified and felt rather sick,

Bessie and Annie, 1924..

Annie and cousin Frank after perfoming in a concert.

but everyone was kind to me, which was very generous of them, considering the damage I had done. My mother had to give me an angry shake in order to make me speak again and I whispered 'Sorry!'

Another cousin called Bert, was a very unusual person because, as a child, he could se visions of ghostly faces peering in through windows. My mother said, 'He'll grow out of it!' And he probably did. When he grew up, he made a Radio set with a cat's whisker and a crystal inside it. It actually worked, because as we stood round it, we could astonishingly hear people's voices. He told me that one day we would not cook in gas ovens but with warm air waves which would make the food hot. I didn't really understand but I realised that he was very clever, but underestimated because he was shy. And of course it has come true.

His father, Uncle Charlie, was kind and always happy. He was tall and walked very straight. Mother said that this was because he had been a soldier in the Boer War and had worn a red uniform. He liked gardening and had a little glass house where he grew tomatoes. They smelled fresh and earthy, a scent which is never there today. When he died I gave him a wreath of flowers and mother helped me to write a card which read 'To the kind gardener with love from Annie', and they put it on his grave. Uncle Charlie was specially interesting because he had two wives – not both at once, of course! His first one was called Agnes – young and pretty with lovely clothes, but she was often ill and sadly died. The second wife, called Emma, was plain and homely like a warm loaf. She was a kindly lady who looked after Uncle Charlie and his two children and everybody liked her. She gave lovely parties at Christmas.

One of my favourite places to visit was my Uncle Frank's baker's shop. My cousin Frank lived there and I used to envy him, having a shop full of fresh loaves and cakes to eat, just when he wanted. The whole house smelled quite delicious. Every morning, by the time my cousin and I were having breakfast, Uncle Frank had already made scores of plain sticky buns, currant buns, cream cakes, meat and potato pies and a whole army of yellow custard pies, sprinkled with nutmeg. He always looked floury, except in the evening when the large ovens were turned off and he removed his white apron.

Another cousin called Winnie was also a very gifted lady. She never married and chose to remain in the same house all her life, with her Mother Annie who was very delicate, with heavy-lidded eyes and a thin, lined face. Their house was one of a row, opposite to an austere grey Congregational Church. That house was a hive of industry, for Winnie never stopped working, even to take a holiday. Not that she considered it to be actual work, because what she did was creative and enjoyable. So after a few years working in the local Co-op, she stayed at home, with her sewing machine whirring continuously.

'There's lots to do,' she would say. 'And if I can make a few shillings to put in my tin box, well that's a bit extra'.

I suspected that the ladies for whom she made dresses, paid her very little, which was all they could afford. Most of them worked in the cotton mills or in the rubber works, or they were older housewives with little money to spare. They all came, as much for the peace and friendliness of that little house, as for the dress-making. And Winnie accepted her lot and wished for no other life. She was my special friend and I called her Winpin.

The house itself reflected her industry. The kitchen shelves were always lined with newspaper or, when she could find any, clean white paper, cut at the edges into pennant shapes. The pots and pans, there for all to see, were clean and shining, well scrubbed at the kitchen sink, which was where we all had our daily wash. Rugs made with pieces of cloth left over from her sewing were everywhere, in all shapes and sizes. For they had cost nothing – only the labour of cutting the cloth and pegging it into a piece of sacking. The oven, part of a kitchen range was black-leaded and shining, with silver hinges and knobs.

There was a large dresser with many drawers crammed so full of things that they were difficult to open and a black horse-hair sofa which I hated because it scratched my bare legs.

Winnie's sewing machine was under the window to catch the light and on it she made dresses, coats, bonnets and hats. One special creation was made for me and I wore it on Walking Day when members of the various Churches paraded through the streets, following the banners. The bonnet was of yellow straw bound with ribbons and festooned with chains of cowslips. It looked very nice, they said, on a little person with red hair.

The staircase was in one corner of the living room, with a curtain at its foot to keep out the draught. At the top was a magic window which overlooked the back yard. It was semi-opaque in the middle, but round the edges were panes of brightly coloured glass which, if you pressed your face close to them, turned the world outside into yellow or red or blue.

There was no bathroom in the house and in order to go to the toilet we had to take a trip down the back yard to a small building, which my Auntie Annie referred to as the petty (but not in Company!) Inside was a wooden plank with a hole cut in it, the walls were white-washed and we had neat squares of newspaper threaded on string behind the door. Sometimes it felt a bit lonely going down there at night and I would make sure that I went with someone else. And while we waited for each other, I would look up at the stars which twinkled clearly, with no street lights to blur the vision. I learned which was the Plough and how to find the Pole Star.

But it was at Winnie's house that I nearly died.

I was happily sucking a sugared almond, a pink sweet with a nut inside and the icing made it smooth and slippery. Suddenly, it slipped down my throat and it stayed there, so that I could hardly breathe. I tried to take in air but I couldn't, and I remember the panic and the whooping noises which I made. Mother turned me upside down and slapped me hard on the back. I felt like a rag doll being whirled about, aware only of the urgent need to breathe. A Doctor lived nearby and Winnie flew to fetch him. My struggle continued and mother's slaps went on, in increasing desperation. Then, just as Winnie and the doctor ran in through the door, mother's efforts succeeded. The sweet was coughed up and only then could I start to cry, while everybody gave me hugs.

My visits to that busy house went on for years. While I was still small, Winnie introduced me to my first fairy – Tinkerbell, who led Peter Pan such a merry dance and I really believed that elves and fairies were around somewhere, hiding in the grasses, or flying in a circling dance with the butterflies. It seemed to me to be a time of perpetual summer.

When I was older, Winnie introduced me to something a little more real – the world of painting. She herself had considerable talent and many of her water colours were hung on the walls. At first we painted while sitting at the kitchen table, while I experimented with fascinating splurges of colour. Then, later, we used to take our art materials and go in search of scenes to paint. At the time, the little town, although grown from a village, still lay in an unspoilt landscape of fields, copses and ponds edged with marsh marigolds. A glimpse of heaven perhaps, as we sat by a stream, where the trees cast their shadows and trailed their long branches of willow and alder. And always the sound of running water. This was a world which I naturally understood.

Sometimes, Winnie and I collected berries, bark and roots which we boiled to make coloured dyes, and used onion skins to produce the delicate yellows, ochres and browns – fairy colours all.

Winnie had another world, uniquely her own, in which I could feel a link but into which I dared not venture too far. Several times she told me that, in the darkness of night, she could hear the gentle slippered sound of feet mounting the stairs and a hand brushing against the landing wall.

'Perhaps it was Auntie Annie coming up to bed,' I said.

'No. She had gone to bed long ago, and anyway she sometimes heard it herself'.

Winnie was never afraid because she said that the person was a friendly soul, whoever she might be, and would wish no one any harm. She also read tea cups, at home or sometimes at parties, when people clustered round and begged her tell them what was in store in the future. They would put real tea in the pot, (no tea bags in those days) pour on boiling water and swish it round. Then it would be poured, still swirling, into tea cups where, when the tea had been drunk, the leaves had settled at the bottom in fascinating patterns. They were a source of great mystery but Winnie knew how to make them give up their secrets. She rarely refused to do it, if she felt truly in touch with whatever magic there was, and used to tell of events in the future in a most amazing way. But sometimes she would say 'No! I can't do it today!' and nothing and nobody could ever make her change her mind.

Once, she told too much and a lady who didn't like what she said, met her in the street and shrieked, 'You're a witch!'

'Did you feel upset?' I asked.

'Not really. If people ask for tea cups to be read, then they have to accept what's there'.

My life in the little town eventually came to an end, like a ball of wool which had used up its thread. I was born a city child and back to the city I would go, but the days which I spent so close to the countryside were never forgotten. I preserved forever the sense of awe and enchantment and of something which often came close to tears.

A kaleidoscope of memories – blackberry picking in autumn, the swings on trees, scary woods where eyes peered, buzzing bees and peacock butterflies, wasps caught in jam-jars laced with sugared water. Knees grazed on uneven pathways, slides were steep and, when I got home, mother complained that my knickers were black!

Sometimes, when alone, I would lie in the ground and gaze through stiff grasses and feel the secret life there. I would smell the earth, while a fat beetle scurried in and out of the flower stems and armies of ants ran in frantic searching.

I learned the names of the wild flowers and loved the sound of their music – Rose Bay Willow Herb, Ragged Robin, Cuckoo Pint, Celandine and the red ones with the impish name of Devil's Buttons. Nettles stung bare legs, spears of prickles scratched hands. Wheat husks pierced our socks, and burrs stuck to our clothes. Spiders spread their webs and dewdrops lay on morning petals.

I loved great drifts of flowers – a sea of Bluebells and white wild Garlic, the hedgerows with Meadow-Sweet and Ragwort and the half-hidden tallness of a Foxglove. Once I adored a whole field of purple Crocuses which grew every year near to the Norman Church and the Vicarage. Known to us as the Crocus Field, it has long since been sacrificed to the diggers and tractors and to the demands of the red brick houses. Only the name remains sadly on a wall of the soulless new road.

Chapter 5

Return to the City

WHEN I WAS EIGHT years old, we returned to Manchester, not to the familiar and friendly remembered house in Alexandra Grove, but to another one, farther out from the city. Mother was delighted and I think that she felt one step up in the world.

'It'll be much better there', she said.

'Why?'

'Well the air is cleaner and the street is not a street! It's a road!'

She looked quite dreamy, 'We shall have a little garden. Two, in fact, at the front and one at the back. We shall have grass and flowers.'

And two trees, I discovered, on arrival. A lime and a Laburnum. I also found out that it had cost six hundred pounds. Which sounded like a fortune to me. I asked where they had got such an enormous amount of money and mother told me that they had borrowed it from the co-op, and had to pay some back each month. It was called a 'Mortgage'.

'By the time you are eighteen, we shall have paid it off.'

From that time on, paying off the mortgage often cropped up in family conversation and the time when it would be repaid was like reaching the promised land.

Like my mother, I was delighted with the new home. Instead of whole rows of terraced houses, they stood out proudly in twos, each pair divided from the neighbours by bushes and hedges. There was a little path leading up to the front door which was a wonderful glass affair with two side panels decorated with red Tulips and curling leaves, the same pattern being repeated on the bay windows. A palace indeed! All the more so, as I discovered that it had electric lighting. I was entranced. No more reaching up to do the central gas light with it's two little chains to raise or lower the flame in the mantle. No more homely flickerings, but a clear steady gleam which penetrated every corner. No more yellow warmth but a cold stare. But how wonderful for it to strike like lightning into darkness, just at the flick of a switch. I was not to know then that it would dominate every house, whole buildings, even whole cities and would eventually set the whole world alight.

The back of the house was even better than the front for it overlooked the side of a railway embankment covered in tall grasses and Willow Herb, (Railway weed they called it). Sometimes the grass caught a hot cinder from the passing trains and burnt black with acid smoke. The trains became my friends. There were two loved ones which journeyed between Manchester and Cheshire. One, a rather blustering slow thing, we called Tommy and another we named Billy. Two carriages ran ahead of Billy's busy little engine and two ran at the back. It couldn't turn round, so it spent its days trundling forwards and backwards.

There were also two special trains by which mother said she could tell the time. At exactly ten minutes past ten, each morning, the Mancunian could be heard thundering in the distance and then, for a few fascinating seconds, it would roar past our house, leaving a trail of smoke and sparks. At exactly nine o'clock in the evening, the Lancastrian would pass, equally loud and swift. These were the two express trains and I loved to see them on winter nights, totally lit from end to end, with silhouettes of passengers inside, on their way to London.

Frosty weather would make the nightly clatter of shunting trains and their haunting whistles, sound loud and clear – the toiling machines which continued to labour when people like myself were safe in bed. Sometimes a locomotive would wheezily drag a whole procession of wagons which would clank and clang while waiting for the signals to change. Occasionally, much less welcoming, was the lowing of cattle and I would feel desperately sorry for the poor creatures imprisoned inside the trucks.

My bedroom was where I kept all my books and toys and there I dreamed day-dreams and sometimes had nightmares. Once, I thought I was being suffocated in a long tunnel and my screams brought mother who found me at the wrong end of the bed, fighting with the blankets.

But, much worse than this, they found me, one night, standing at the top of the stairs, fast asleep.

'You were walking in your sleep,' said mother next day.

'I don't remember.'

'Perhaps you were having another dream.'

I did this once more and after that, they decided that steps must be taken to keep me safe. Father screwed a large metal hook and eye between the door and the lintel, so that it allowed the door to remain a jar. I couldn't reach it, so it solved the problem for a while and I don't remember feeling worried about being locked in because I felt secure.

My bedroom window looked down upon a small square garden which was tended happily by my father. In June it was smothered in pink roses which had spread from a cutting all over the back fence. He grew Stocks, Cat-Mint, Nasturtiums and Marguerites which always had smudges from the passing trains. I loved the names 'Love-in-a-Mist', 'Lad's Love'. 'Columbine' and the tiny yellow flowered ground creeper which, father said, rejoiced in the name of 'Mind your own business'. Mother didn't work in the garden, because she had so much else to do, but she was always happy to go out and pick the flowers.

'I grow 'em,' said father, 'And she picks 'em!'

Mother had an aptitude for arranging flowers and in summer, we always had vases of greenery and colour. Her favourite flowers were lilies -of-the-valley. I used to climb over the fence near to the notice on the embankment which said 'Trespassers will be prosecuted.', and pick Rose Bay and Willow Herb. But it never lasted and ended up in a disappointing droop in the jam jar. I once went picking Bluebells in a wood, but on the whole, I decided very early that wild flowers were best left in peace to grow in the sun and the rain.

We had two neighbours, one large family on one side, and a single lady on the other. She was very quiet but the family was a noisy one and we could hear their piano, thumping through the wall. The mother was called Mrs. Owen and she had a husband who could only hear if you shouted very loud indeed. He was smart and gentlemanly, unlike his wife who was anything but a lady with a very red face and bad manners. She was a very inquisitive person.

'A right busy-body!' mother would remark, as we saw her peering from behind her curtains at the comings and goings of all the neighbours. Once, mother said she was common and that she didn't 'fit in', so I concluded that she didn't like Mrs. Owen very much. She wasn't very good at looking after her money either, and she would appear at our back door on Monday mornings to borrow a cup of sugar and could she also borrow a two-shilling piece, or maybe half-a-crown – 'Until Friday' she would say. Mother always obliged but did not approve. I often wondered what Mr. Owen would say if he knew that his wife was always coming round to borrow money. Actually, she did always pay it back on Friday (until Monday came round once more and she would borrow it again). I thought that it wasn't fair because mother needed it herself.

Our other neighbour, Miss Howe, was a very fashionable lady and always had smart clothes. Sometimes she would pass some discarded dresses over the fence to mother, who would turn then into blouses for herself and frocks for me. She once made me a very special green dress in which I felt like a princess and I boasted about it to a friend, Dorothy, who lived up the road.

'It's all soft and silky,' I said, 'It's called Angel skin.'

'Angel skin! Never heard of it!'

'Well my dress is made of it,' I protested.

'I wouldn't like that!' she said scornfully. 'Who wants to look like an angel, and anyway, angels have white clothes.'

'Don't take any notice,' mother said, when I told her.

My parents had various friends who used to call and sometimes she would organise a little supper, preceded by some games of whist. They would all sit round a little table, warm and cosy, next to a cheerful fire in our front room.

'Come and play with us, said mother. 'You can play whist very well.'

'But I don't like it,' I said. I considered that cards were only time – fillers on days when the weather was bad, and I could imagine nothing worse then having to remain solemn for at least two hours, with everyone stiffly correct and few smiles exchanged, if any. But I was always persuaded to join them at supper time, because my mother's Lancashire Hot Pots were quite wonderful!

The Adams family were polite whist players, very genteel and subdued and they played cards with unenthusiastic murmuring, and no obvious urge to win. Nice people, but I waited and listened and never heard an excited word or a peal of laughter. Mrs. Adams always wore blue dresses, jackets, coats, hats, scarves – nothing so shocking as pink or as dismal as black.

Sometimes we paid visits ourselves to the houses of old friends. One family, the Evans', was quite musical and I was even persuaded to learn the violin (but not for long.) Mr. Evans used to knit and do some housework, my mother told me, her voice inferring that she did not approve of such a state of affairs. Having tea at people's houses was not always satisfying. I seemed to spend many hours in merely being polite and wishing that it was time to go home, not surprising, because I was only nine.

I found it very much more interesting when I went to visit my friend Dorothy and we knew each other for many years. We each had a dolls house. Mine had a verandah at the front, but I was rather jealous because it was much smaller than Dorothy's.

It rankled for a while and then I persuaded Father to make me an extension. He was certainly not a carpenter, but he went out and bought some plywood, finally producing an extra bedroom and a little kitchen. I didn't mind the fact that the two roof-tops did not meet and that the windows were not quite straight. I gave him a big hug.

Anyway, Mr. & Mrs. Willoughby were very pleased with it, because their family kept growing. These were the small dolls with moveable arms and legs, made of a material called celluloid. I chose the name Willoughby because it sounded stylish, better than Dorothy's family of dolls who were simply called Clarke. They all had separate identities, quarrelled or had parties and sometimes had a terrible accident like having a squashed-in head. Big dolls were put away and rarely played with; for the two little families led much more interesting lives.

At first, Dorothy and I went to different schools and so I found a new friend called Ruby. Our school was quite a distance away and so we had to go there on a tram which cost a half-penny each way. We boarded it at West Point, a rather grand name which denoted a small area with a tiny park and several shops. It was also a terminus for the 38 tram and we used to watch it lurching and swaying towards us, knowing that the exciting part was to come – its turn-about! We would stand in the tram shelter and watch the passengers alighting. Then the driver would climb down from the front and seize the rope attached to the trolley, run with it to the back and fix it, with a flurry of sparks, to the overhead wires. It was now ready to set off again, the way it had come. We used to sit at the front and watch the driver swinging the large brass handle which steered it down the tram lines, his foot kicking at a cog-wheel to make it stop.

There was also a conductor, as cheerful as the driver was solemn and he used to punch a hole in a little ticket in exchange for the half-penny fare. He would chat to me, as we were swaying along and he said that he'd been in the war and had met some Germans.

'You know that long wall which we pass, down Moseley Road – well that's where we kept Germans during the war, Prisoners they were'.

'Who were Germans?' I asked.

'People with a funny way of speaking. They were our enemies – you know – the 'other side'!'

'You mean that you quarrelled all the time!'

'Some quarrel!' he said. 'We were all fighting. Every fit man there was!'

'What was it like – the war?' I said.

He paused. 'Well – let's say I was one of the lucky ones!' Then he said 'Tell you what! I'll count in German!'

I listened while he confidently recited 'Ine, Swine, Drine, Fear, Foomf, Seeven, Act, Noin, Zane, Elf, Swelf! That's one to twelve!'

I know now that he would never have been understood by any German, but at the time it seemed a great triumph.

'Thank you very much!' I said. Then I repeated the numbers until I could say them exactly like he did.

'I can speak German!' I boasted to mother, when I got home. She was not to know that it wasn't exactly accurate and was very impressed. So was father, because he didn't know German either.

Then he said, 'I can say something foreign too! Listen to this!' and he sang in an up-and-down tune:

'Arry Inchy Ane-she-ah,
Picanniny Annie-ah,
Inga-binga bunny-ah
Down a linchy lane-eeah!

'How's that then!'

It didn't seem to matter that nobody had the vaguest idea what it meant, but I loved it and made him repeat it many times, even though I could say it myself.

Ruby and I were always glad when school finished and sometimes, before going across the road to wait for our tram, we used to visit the little Toffee-shop which was there to tempt the children. We did nothing more than gaze in the window and only went in when one of us had a penny to spend, which wasn't often. But one day, I hit upon a great idea.

'I know!' I exclaimed. 'Let's walk home and then we can spend our half-penny tram fare on toffee!'

'Let's!' said Ruby.

So we pushed open the little door with its tinkling bell, and spent several fascinating minutes in choosing what we could buy with a half-penny each. A Luckybag? Too dear! They cost a penny. A packet of Kali with a tube for sucking it up? A gobstopper? Or a few aniseed balls? In the end, we settled for a coil of shiny black Spanish liquorice with a tiny sweet in the centre, one each. We made them last until we reached West Point, where Ruby went one way and I went the other. Mother was waiting at the door 'And where do you think you've been, young lady?'

'Walking home.' I answered sheepishly.

'Walking home! And who pays for all the shoe-leather you've worn out! And – where's the half-penny?'

'That wouldn't buy much shoe leather!' I said, playing for time.

'I'll not be having any cheek, lady!' and for that I got a slap on the legs.

'Well, where is it ?'

'Haven't got it'

'What did you say? Haven't got it! Have you lost it or swallowed it? Come on! Let's be hearing!'

I had to confess of course and, after another onslaught of scolding, mother turned her back on me until Father came home from work and had to be told the whole miserable story. I think, deep down, he had a tiny bit of sympathy – maybe because he'd done a few naughty things when he was a boy (although it was a bit difficult to imagine!)

'Umph!' grunted Mother, when he failed to fly into a rage. 'That's right! Leave all the bringing up to me! She's not going to be spoiled if I have anything to do with it !'

Her lips were pressed into a thin line which always happened if she became angry.

But next day, it all seemed to be forgiven, and a week later, mother grudgingly said 'Your Father and me we've been talking. You can have a penny a week to spend! But don't waste it on rubbish! D'you hear?'

I heard and I was delighted!

My new Manchester school was enormous. It was built of red brick with a grey playground and railings surrounding it. Nothing grew in the black soil of empty flower-beds except for the odd weary bush. There were two separate entrances, one for the girls and the one for the boys. Inside, the walls were half-tiled in dark green and there was a great deal of brown paint which made the place look dull and dead. If I built a school, I used to say to myself, I would paint it all in sunshine yellow so that all the children would be bright and cheerful and learn a lot better. I was right of course, as I later found out!

I was put into Standard 2B but later promoted to Standard 2A because I could read, write and do my sums quite easily. But there was one thing that I could not do! Father had tried to teach me but I still could not tell the time. I never understood why, except that the more I tried, the more in a panic I got – until I simply accepted it and stopped trying. Then there came one dreadful morning which jolted me out of my laziness, or stubbornness, or whatever it was. I was sitting in my desk, day-dreaming as usual, because I had finished my page of sums and was looking forward to a pleasing array of ticks.

'Annie!' the teacher's voice came sharply. 'As you seem to have finished, go into the hall and check the time. My watch has stopped.' My eyes widened in fright and my heart was pounding. (I hoped it wouldn't stop!)

What would the teacher say if he knew I couldn't tell the time! The panic got worse. I climbed reluctantly out of my desk and walked slowly to the classroom door.

'And be quick about it!'

I entered the hall and stood in front of the large round clock, high up on the wall. Teachers' voices and the murmur of children sounded as if they were far away. The clock gazed back at me, with its two fingers, one large and one small. The large numbers went blurred and would not help me at all. Should I run out of school or visit the toilet? (I wanted to go anyway!)

Then help came in the form of a senior girl who was crossing the hall.

'Please!' I beseeched, 'Can you tell me the time?' She looked at me curiously.

'It's twenty five past ten' she said, 'and you should know that!'

I broke into a relieved smile. 'Just making sure!' I said.

I don't remember ever learning to read all those secrets on the clock, but one day it happened, I just could.

But the same teacher had not finished with me yet! We had our story books for class reading.

'Come out Annie, and read page four'.

Well, I read it aloud and thought that I had done it rather nicely.

'What about letter H?' said the teacher, frowning. 'We must have a little practice. Right? Now repeat after me – 'Harry Hoggart holds his head high! Say it six times!'

The other children stared until my face felt hot and one or two began to whisper.

'Again!' snapped the teacher.

I could have killed Harry Hoggart, whoever he was, and I crept back to my desk, knowing I was too old to cry. I guess the exercise must have done the trick because I went around breathing aitches all over the place, even when they were not there.

School felt much better when I went up into Standard 3A where we had a gentle teacher called Miss Bell. I would have done anything for Miss Bell, because I knew she wouldn't have me repeating Harry Hoggart six times. She used to arrive at school every morning, crossing the playground always dressed in blue. She had a fox fur draped around her shoulders and it had stiff little legs hanging down, a wicked snout and gleaming eyes. But on one occasion I saw it more closely and it did not look half so ferocious nor, with a bald patch or two, did it look so splendid.

One day she told us to prepare a little talk on any subject we liked and we were to give it in front of the class the following week.

'Think about it now' she said 'and write down on this piece of paper what you would like to choose.'

I loved the whole idea and I sat there in my desk, thinking hard, while a fly buzzed up and down the classroom window. The girl next to me wrote PETS and a boy poked me in the back and whispered 'TRAINS'. Little Miss Cleverclogs, of course, had to go one better! I wrote down PYRAMIDS.

Standard 3 – Annie (middle of back row) aged eight.

When my turn came, the following week, I drew a diagram of a pyramid on the blackboard and told everybody about the mummies and coffins which I had seen in the Manchester Museum, as well as the great dead Pharaoh himself. I can't remember whether the class was suitably impressed but I think Miss Bell was pleased.

It was about this time that I began to have trouble with my eyes. I couldn't see the blackboard too clearly and had to sit on the front row. I said nothing to mother and father but they noticed that there were things in the distance which I couldn't read. So father took me to an Eye Specialist and I had to wear glasses. I don't remember being too upset about it.

That came later, in my teenage years, when I very much minded looking like a tawny owl. I was dreading the thought of being called Specky four Eyes but I never was. My parents could only afford the cheapest frames, although my Father made sure that the lenses were exactly correct. They were very round, made of tortoiseshell, with gold pieces which curled round my ears and made them sore. But it was good to see clearly. Everything seemed nearer and darker, especially the black tree trunks.

At the end of that school year, my Mother said 'How would you like to go to that new School they're building? It's only round the corner. No need to go in the tram.' I thought about it. No more lurching tram, no more Toffee Shop and no more Ruby, because she was staying where she was. I wasn't sure, but they were giving me the choice.

'Dorothy's going. I've seen her mother.'

'All right then!' I said. 'I'll go.'

So it was, that for one year, when I turned ten, I attended a brand new school built in what was then a totally new design, possibly one of the first. The classrooms all opened out onto verandahs with French windows which let in fresh air in summer. We could see the playing fields and the boys playing football. There were no dark green tiles, or brown paint and the walls were painted cream. Even the teachers must have been pleased.

My teacher was Miss McMinn, a holy terror, people said she was, with her piercing eyes and ram-rod back. She always held a ruler which she used to rap smartly on the top of a piano which stood in a corner. She seemed all right to me. We got on well and she even gave me a book prize for a composition which I wrote called 'Under the Sea'. Although she was one of the strictest teachers I had known and had that fierce reputation, I never remember that she used her ruler to tap knuckles (in those days it was accepted that children could be caned – usually only the boys).

All day long, from the time we stood stiffly in our desks and chorused 'Good morning Miss McMinn!' we were worked like slaves. She had the means of making any would-be idlers mend their ways, mainly through sarcastic words and glaring eyes. We all worked in total silence. There was no whispering, no pulling of pig-tails, no gazing through the windows.

But there came a time when her pupils, subdued and repressed, had to express their high-spirits somehow, and one day circulating among the school population like wild fire, was a rhyme about Miss McMinn, brief but telling, I guess that the poor lady never suspected that, under her pupils' meek exteriors, lurked something which they knew and she didn't.

It went like this, repeated in a sing-song voice:

'Miss McMinn
Tall and thin!
Nanny goat's whiskers
On her chin!'

That was all! A little unkind perhaps but not so very wicked.

It was in this my last year in Junior School that I decided to be an author. I used to retreat into my own world as I began to write 'Ruffles of Oak Wood', basing the title on my favourite story book, 'Tuffy the Tree Elf'. But Ruffles had adventures of his own and I got as far as Chapter Six, with drawings to match. Father let me use his old type-writer which had a sticky ink ribbon and scores of hinged arms which came out and struck the paper when a letter key was pressed. I slowly typed out my story, using two fingers on each hand (which is why I never learned to type properly). I have it still, held together with a rusty pin and it might have been finished, had not a new teacher in the following year poured scorn upon the elves and fairies and the trees with secret doorways. She read to the class a similar piece about my back garden, where the trees were dancing together, adding heavy sarcasm and a final admonition to write plainly. I never wrote like that again, just keeping to the simple and the factual, in order to pass exams. It was heart-rending at the time but I knew it was good advice, honestly given. Incredibly I kept my respect for that teacher.

One day, a boy in my class was kept in at playtime by Miss McMinn, leaving him to struggle, while she went off to have her coffee. I think he had not been to successful at working out how much water would fill a bath in five minutes. He was a quiet shy boy called Geoffrey and I felt really sorry for him so I lurked by the verandah window to show my sympathy. Then, after school, while walking home, he and another boy, Tony Lewis, followed Dorothy and I with a shuffling of feet, treading on heels, low whistling, and, on our part, much giggling. Nothing was said and finally we all went our separate ways.

But that started it all. Dorothy decided that she liked Tony and said so.

'You're sweet on him!' I said.

'Well! What about you then! I've seen you looking at Geoffrey Fernyhough!'

I blushed, an affliction which was to plague me from then on. I looked at him often, after that, at his rather peaky face with two dark eyes, at his desk-worn shiny pants and his jerseys with neatly-darned holes. I couldn't help thinking that he was a wee bit skinny for a lad and maybe not as tall as I was. Tony Lewis, on the other hand, was fair, good-looking and would no doubt grow up into a handsome young man. But never mind! I felt that, somehow, Geoffrey needed me.

On the other hand, I thought, with a pang of chagrin, what had I to offer? A mane of ginger hair, blue eyes behind my horn-rimmed glasses and a timid glance. Oh yes! I did have a set of brains in good order, but that was no advantage when Geoffrey was, to put it kindly, a little bit slow. But nice.

When I got home, I looked at myself in the mirror and tried taking off my glasses. But if I didn't wear them, Geoffrey would be sitting in a kind of blur, across the classroom! So they remained. However, I did feel glad that at least I didn't squint like Amy Jones.

The next day, I risked a few sidelong glances at him, where he was sitting, chewing his pen or grinding it painfully into his exercise book. In country dancing he chose me for a partner and I held his dry horny hand and dreamed about it through the English lesson.

That afternoon, while we were all sitting, heads down over our reading books, I took a terrible risk. I sent Geoffrey a note across the classroom, hoping that he could read it and would know it was from me. It was passed, with practised secrecy, from hand to hand, until it was smirkingly put on Geoffrey's desk, fully opened, half-read and finger-marked. I can't even remember what it said.

So the term passed and the highlight was to be the Christmas party. We were all in a state of great excitement as a Christmas tree arrived in the Big Hall and classrooms were allowed their own festoons of tinsel and a few balloons. It suddenly became very important to have a new party dress, and mother, to give her credit, rose to the occasion. I came home, one day to see some velvet cut out ready do sew. Another of Miss Howe's handouts.

'It was a cocktail dress,' said mother.

'What's cocktails?'

'Something people drink at parties. Your father says they're poison.'

'Do people drop down and die?' I asked horrified.

'Not as bad as that, but they aren't good for you.'

The dress, when finished, was quite wonderful, with a small lace collar in white, and velvet-covered buttons. I wondered what Geoffrey would be wearing instead of those darned jerseys he always wore. I imagined us playing Musical Chairs, or sitting next to each other at supper, delirious over the cakes and jellies.

But nothing happened as I had dreamed and I painfully found out what it was like to have a huge disappointment which left a hollow feeling deep inside. As it turned out, Geoffrey and I saw each other very briefly. He looked very uncomfortable in a button-tight jacket and shiny boots, while the other kids looked quite unlike their everyday selves. They thumped round the hall, with shiny faces, curled-up hair and clean socks, under the streamers and the balloons.

Suddenly, father loomed in the doorway, looking stern and out of place. I couldn't believe it!

'We have to go,' he said. 'Your grandma Sarah has died and we're going to catch the train.'

I said nothing because I was too numb to speak,

And so it was, that, like Cinderella, I had to return to grey reality, with all the Christmas magic gone, along with my dreams. Mother was waiting at home and I put on my thick cloth coat which sat incongruously on top of my velvet dress, and a woolly bonnet was rammed down over my ears to keep out the freezing cold.

When we reached Victoria Station, fog had descended, a choking yellow mantle, which mingled with the smoke from the engines and it made me cough and sneeze. When all the passengers were packed in, the train doors were banged with rhythmic clangs, as the porter moved down the platform. 'All aboard!' His whistle blew, his green flag waved and we were off, steaming with a great clatter of wheels into the December darkness. It matched the mood I was in.

The journey ended and there was the familiar sign at the little station – LEYLAND. After a short walk down a steep brew we found ourselves in Grandma Sarah's kitchen, where a great fire was roaring up the chimney, the most cheerful thing in the room. Various uncles and aunts were sitting about, dressed in black and looking glum. Even our arrival did not unduly disturb the solemnity. 'That's because they mustn't waken the dead,' I said to myself, remembering something which I had read. It all felt strange and rather creepy.

There was Auntie Janie, my father's sister and one of my favourite people because she had grown very fat through laughing so much. But tonight she looked quite different, her plump cheeks drooping down. Uncle Walter was there too (my father's brother), another jolly man who was now serious and solemn, and his wife Auntie Rose who always clicked her teeth when smiling. But no clicking tonight. Next to them was my father's youngest brother, Frank, who had retained a subdued smile and looked handsome with fair curly hair. His wife, Aunt Nellie, looked rather nice, I thought, in her black dress, as so she ought, for she had once been the May Queen, chosen for being the prettiest girl in the village. That was when, they said, Uncle Frank had fallen in love with her and had chased her round the Maypole. At least, that was what I imagined and I thought it wonderfully romantic. Later they had a little daughter called Edna, another cousin for me!

I had to go round and kiss everybody, which, shy as I was, I hated doing. I won't make any child of mine go kissing, I thought. Auntie Janie looked at my hair and I knew she was thinking of her eldest sister, the Annie who had died.

'You look bonnie', she said.

Uncle Walter patted my head and I could see that his thumb was indeed missing, the result of a terrible accident with a saw, in the woodyard where he worked. My father looked stern and very much in charge of his family. 'He's doing his duty,' I thought.

Then I heard his voice.

'Annie! Are you listening?' (How often was I to hear that, over the years!) 'I think you ought to go upstairs and see your grandmother.'

I grew rigid with fright. I didn't, just didn't, want to climb up the narrow steep stairs to look at her lying on the bed, all stiff and not moving. I was terrified that she might open her eye – her good eye, because the other was blinded by a pin, which had flown up when she was shaking a rug. All her eye drained away, so someone told me. I shivered.

However, mother glancing at me with some understanding, saw that I was upset, although I felt that she had mistaken terror for sorrow that poor Sarah had died. I felt quite unmoved, to tell the truth, for I had seen her rarely and so I didn't really know her at all.

'Leave her be,' said mother and they let me remain downstairs. Then I begun to feel sorry for myself. A tear rolled silently down.

'Poor me!' I thought.

'Poor Geoffrey' and then, as an after-thought,

'Poor Grandmother.'

That was the end of Geoffrey and me, for when January came and a new term began, his family had moved away and I never saw him again.

Father's youngest brother Frank, who looked handsome with curly hair.

Edna, another cousin for me.

Frank's wife Nellie, chosen as May Queen.

Chapter 6

Four Aspects of the Same Man

Dutiful Father

T ISN'T EVERYBODY who has several fathers rolled into one, but looking back, this is how it seemed to me. There was, for instance, the father of pronounced opinions, of stubbornness and upright air, who could be frighteningly stern at times. For instance, there was one occasion when I had stayed out playing too long and it was beginning to get dark. When I arrived home, I dashed in to find father standing with his back to the fireplace, looking thunderously stern. My mother, for once, never said a word, while I was given what they called a thorough 'telling off'. But it gave me quite a fright because I hated raised voices and after that, I never dared to come home late.

There was also another father, a respected and trusted worker, yet another with a sense of humour and one more who loved animals. But I always found him kind and I loved him without question. As I grew older, I inevitably began to re-evaluate the person who had been the centre of my world. By the time I had reached my teen years he had set himself up as the guardian of my moral upbringing. His method was to pour scorn upon any deviation from the 'rules' or from the straight and narrow, mainly dictated by his own strict upbringing and early privations. He would grimly warn of the consequences if those rules were not kept and would launch into a condemnation of those who did not do so, especially those who drank beer and the women who painted their faces!

An early photograph of my parents' wedding in 1911 as they posed stiffly and without smiles, shows a handsome young man and apparently one who had strong ideals.

'He looks like a parson!' mother would say. 'He should have gone into the Church!' And father, with his serious expression and stiff white collar, never disagreed.

Once, he had a photograph taken, which showed several images of himself, set at different angles and reflected by hidden mirrors. All aspects of the same man.

He proudly carried the name of Harold Clinton and he was particularly

Photograph of father reflected in mirrors.

fond of the Clinton, although he had no idea how he came by it. His Father, Hugh, an Insurance Collector, had died relatively young, leaving his wife Sarah with four children. It became a time of frugality, when every farthing had to be counted. Clothes were shared as 'hand-me-downs', passed from one child to another and many were the embarrassing occasions when one child had to appear in trousers too

Father, as a little boy, backrow, last on right.

long, baggy at the waist and a jersey that was big enough for two. Poor little souls – no wonder there was little to smile about.

When my father's eldest sister died tragically at eighteen years of age it wasn't long before my father appointed himself as head of the family, even though he was only eleven! He began to attend school only for part time and took on the job of errand boy at a local mill so that he could contribute his meagre wages to the family every Friday. He was once chosen to play football in the village team, but after a rough game or two, he gave it up. 'If I had broken a leg' he explained to me, 'I wouldn't have been able to work you see!'

Duty was duty and he was to take it seriously for the rest of his life.

He became a staunch member of the Wesleyan Chapel and it was there that eventually he met my mother who used to sing in the choir. The Wesleyans were a strict bunch. Drinking and dancing were forbidden, neither were they allowed to wash clothes on a Sunday! Father signed the Pledge promising total abstinence from alcoholic liquor and got his young sister and two young brothers to sign it as well. When he married, mother had to do the same and they kept the promise for the rest of their lives. As for me, he made me understand that demon drink was a terrible evil which was responsible for all the unhappiness in England.

My parents were married in 1911 and Father, soon afterwards, applied for, and obtained, an office job in Manchester which was, he said, 'a great improvement' on the 'dead-end' type of work in the cotton mill. Together they journeyed to the strange unfamiliar city and began life in Alexandra Grove where I was born and a union which lasted forty eight years.

His office work was associated with the Temperance Movement and he no doubt obtained it through his early exemplary act of having signed the Pledge. There was a growing number of such societies during the period which followed the first Great War, and especially in the large over-crowded cities where drink was freely available and easily obtained. Out of that post-war generation, there also emerged a whole culture of people, both men and women, who laboured to encourage education, to relieve the poverty and the social injustices of that period. They contributed something stable and morally strong. Statues of such people were prominently displayed on large plinths in our city squares, their names being gradually forgotten with the passage of time.

The effects of drink were plain to see if you went into the poorer parts of the city. The men who spent their Friday night wages in the public houses, left their unfortunate wives to struggle against grinding poverty, while the Pawn Brokers did a roaring trade. The kinder among the shop-keepers allowed a desperate woman to take groceries 'on tick' or as some people put it, 'on the slate'. A neighbour who was lucky enough to have some food might share it, rather than see a child go hungry. Clothes were little more than rags and often there was no money for shoes. The earnest and well-meaning members of a Temperance Society did their best to steer the drinkers towards more sober habits, usually without success. So the children were targeted as being more amenable and more easily influenced.

Thus my father as a Brother in the Sons of Temperance and my Mother as a Sister, made their contribution, taking me along with them; somewhat reluctantly. They took charge of a children's' meeting in Hulme, an area which was later destroyed in another great war, by incendiaries, doodle bugs and one enormous land mine. Each Tuesday evening, we boarded a tram and then walked, in sun, rain or snow, through a maze of cobbled streets with grey houses whose shabby front doors opened out onto the pavements – packed-together buildings with squalid passageways. Sometimes a pale face would press against a curtainless window, and if it was fine, a few dirty children would play in the gutters, while mothers watched from front door-steps. People walked expressionless in shabby clothes, the women clutching at grey or black shawls.

I was always hurried past the Public Houses, the 'dens of iniquity' as father called them, although I had no idea what he meant. But they could not entirely be ignored with their wide-open doors, red and gold paint and the sickly smell which cam from inside. The names were fascinating if meaningless, Dog and Partridge, Rose and Crown, Hanging Gate and Kings Head. (We had a king at the time called George, but why just his head!)

Children of all ages came to our meetings, ragged, unwashed and runny-nosed. Mother used to thump out a hymn tune on an old piano with missing keys and sometimes told them a story, while father turned them all into Cadets of Temperance who promised solemnly not to drink. 'Remember what happens if your father spends his wages in the pub!' (He could have added, but of course he never did, 'when he comes home drunk, half-crazy and with a handy fist!')

All this made me quite upset and I must have sat still in solemn silence, wondering why I was there. The little room was in a basement and was windowless and had a dreadful smell, a mixture of unwashed clothes and fumes from an old gas radiator. In winter, however, that smelly little room must have been a weekly refuge and possibly one of the few times that the kids felt really warm. I understood part of this, yet felt uncomfortable, without knowing why. I think I was half aware of the gap between those children and ourselves, along with a vague feeling that there was a mite of condescension in all this. At the same time, I knew that it was really kind of my parents who gave up all those evenings, doing their dutiful best.

If the stirrings of philanthropy remained dormant in me, the physical effects were quite clear! Often, after a homeward journey in a jolting tram, I began to feel sick and sometimes was! It seemed as if the gas fumes and the smells of poverty hung about in my memory as if they were still actually there. Mother used to say, 'Oh, you'll get used to it!'

'We've got to do our best' said father.

And we did. For years.

Other people, far more influential than father, were, at this time, working politically. They campaigned for shorter opening hours in the Public Houses. Fewer hours of opening, fewer pints to be drunk, they reasoned! But it didn't quite work out like that, for often the men would send out their women for a jug of beer to drink at home. They carried it through the streets with a corner of an apron to keep it clean, not that it mattered too much.

Even King George was involved in all this, because someone wrote a letter to him at Buckingham Palace and the reply came, giving his 'gracious permission' for his health to be drunk in water.

Another of Father's duties was to attend adult meetings – dreary affairs in a depressing hall, where long-faced men and women, covered in silver chains, were seated on a high platform facing an audience of unadorned Brothers and Sisters. I could tell that they were the important ones and I was fascinated by their strange titles, Patrons or Patriarchs. If they had been on a platform for years and then retired, they became Past Grand Worthy Patriarchs. I wondered if they were pleased with this odd privilege, especially as the silver chains became longer and more ornate.

Their efforts were, without doubt, truly commendable but to a small girl they spoke in long tedious riddles. I would pull at mother's sleeve.

'When are we having tea and biscuits?'

'Be quiet!'

'I can hear the cups and saucers rattling'.

'Ssh!'

'Can I read my book?'

'No, you can't!' snapped mother.

I reached such a height of exasperation that I resolved to ask father if, next time, I could stay at home with the dog.

The following year, father told me that he would like me to enter for the Cadet examination.

'If you do well, they give you a medal' he said 'and a prize'.

That settled it! I said 'Right-ho!'

So father brought home a little booklet all about alcohol and the terrible things it did to your body, like destroying your liver and addling your brains. You would get drunk, stagger about and sing in a cracked voice. It made me think.

I memorised the little book from cover to cover and all I had to do on the day of the examination was to spill out chunks of text and throw in a few diagrams for good measure. It was easy.

I got 100 marks and a bronze medal, as well as a Brownie Box camera for a prize. It seemed to me rather a good stroke of business and over the next three years I accumulated other medals and more prizes, the last one being a guitar which I could not play because the metal string cut into my fingers. If father had realised what a calculating little minx I was, I guess he would not have been so pleased.

One day, my mother, also with an eye towards a business deal, bought two penny raffle tickets from a neighbour. To her great delight she found that she had won a prize. The pleasure turned rather sour, when she discovered that it was a bottle of whisky. Father got very angry. 'You shouldn't have bought the tickets!' he told mother.

'Well, I didn't know about the whisky'.

'What's whisky?' I asked.

Father declared that he would not, most definitely not, have it in the house. Then he changed his mind. We had a very serious ceremony, the three of us and the dog, round the kitchen sink, while father poured it down the plug-hole. It made a rather interesting glug-glugging noise.

'There!' he said. 'Nobody's going to get drunk on that!'

'It has a funny smell' I said.

Jolly Father

Jolly Father appeared at Christmas, when everything was happy and warm and full of laughter, because that is how I remember it.

We used to go back to the little village where he was born, that village which was now rapidly developing into a busy industrial town and where all my relatives still lived. We stayed with Winnie, my ever-busy cousin, and on Christmas Eve we would arrive out of the night with frozen feet, blowing out our cheeks with the cold and glad to be in that cheerful room, with its fire leaping in the black-leaded grate. The oven had been prepared for the next day shining with anticipation of its task of roasting the goose. There were the rag-rugs, the gleaming posts and pans and vases of holly with red berries. There was no money for a tree, nor for tinsel and baubles, nor did we miss them. Christmas then did not reflect the commercialism of today.

My cousin Bessie had long ago given me water-tight information! 'There is no Father Christmas you know. It's your mum and dad'. But that did not prevent me from hanging up my stocking, (actually, one of father's socks!) and there it was on Christmas morning, an orange and nuts in the toe, bulging with presents. Carols were merry on the wireless as parcels were opened and all their secrets revealed.

We sat down to our Christmas dinner with its array of steaming vegetables – buttery carrots, brussels sprouts and a jug of luscious gravy. We all watched while the goose, still trussed with string, oozing juices and surrounded by sausages, was carried in. Cousin Winnie, for reasons known only to herself, burst into song. 'Bringing in the cheese!' I used to feel so sorry for Auntie Annie who could eat none of it, for she had a weak stomach which would accept only the smallest portion of rice pudding. She was dreadfully thin. She looked at us earnestly through gold-rimmed glasses, nodded and smiled as we gorged ourselves until we could eat no more, and watched with quiet approval when one of us (and strangely enough, it was always me) found a threepenny bit in the pudding.

The days which followed were full of Aunts, Uncles and jolly Cousins, singing carols round the piano, bursting balloons, gobbling trifle and mince pies or playing games. Father came into his own and was in great demand as the organiser of 'Spin the Platter', 'Winking' and 'Guess the Proverb' of arranging the forfeits and awarding the prizes. Then my cousins would mob my father begging him to show them his magic tricks for which he was famous.

'Awh! Go on Uncle Harold! Let's have the skeleton!'

The lights would be put out and the skeleton would appear in the firelight, jogging on an invisible string and everyone pretended that they didn't know how it was done!

'What about the performing pig!'

'The Magic Box please!'

No-one could open the Magic Box except father and he kept that as an unsolved secret. Then there was the straw finger which fitted over your own and would never come off, until father did it. At supper, the plates would mysteriously jump about and finally, there would come the best trick of all.

'Have you bought your magic machine?'

'Can we get it?'

'My turn first!'

Then it would appear, a little square box, with 2 batteries inside and two metal handles to hold, always with great squeals of laughter.

'Ow! Ouch! It's electricity!'

The boys liked it better than the girls. 'Well, we're men!' they said.

Another strange event always had to take place, by popular demand, which father declared was the result of science and not of magic. Perhaps it was, because it always seemed to work and even father did not know why. A person would sit in a chair and four others would place their hands on his head and press down.

'Ouch! That's too hard!' The victim would say.

'Has to be pressed hard' declared father.

After a moment or two came the exciting bit. Two 'pressers' would place one finger under the knee of the man in the chair and two would place a finger under his arm-pit. Up he would go, towards the ceiling and everybody would cheer. He was up for only a few seconds but the astounding feat was complete, witnessed by all. It was the high-light of the evening and father was considered to be quite the miracle man.

Father, the Dog Expert

Well, he wasn't really, but he loved dogs and they responded to him. He had been very found of Nap, our Alsation and I know that he was very distressed when he had to let him go. Then he had the chance to own a very attractive black Labrador puppy. Actually, she was supposed to be mine, but knowing how he felt about dogs, I shared her with father and allowed him to be the one who took her for walks, cleaned up any mess, or scolded her if she was not obedient.

She came from my Uncle Walter who wrote to father offering the puppy. 'For Annie's birthday' he had written.

'I'll have it!' I said promptly.

'What do you think mother?' asked father.

'She'll grow too big'.

'Not so big!' I exclaimed. 'She won't be as big as a St. Bernard'.

Nan.

'Who'll feed her?' asked mother.

'I will!' I said, jumping up and down.

'Humph! That'll be the day!'

'We've got to have it!' was father's final word.

And so we did. We took the train to Uncle Walter's house and found him in his shop, surrounded by buckets, mops and saucepans.

Auntie Rose was there too (of the famous clicking teeth and perpetual smile) She had also dyed her hair very black, which my mother thought was quite wicked. We chose a plump black puppy with a beautiful soft coat and I thought that I'd never seen such a beautiful creature. We put her inside a carpet bag with two handles and she travelled home with us to Manchester, sleeping all the way. She never even raised her head when we gave up our train tickets to the collector at the station.

'Father!' I said. 'Should she have had a ticket too?'

'Too late now!' said father as we hurried on.

We called her Nan and immediately she became an important member of the family. Mother decided to be responsible for feeding her and father took her walks. As we grew up together I used to talk to her about all my joys and sorrows and there were a few times when life became disappointing and I would bury my face in her fur and cry. She got on well with everybody except when she sneaked handkerchiefs out of pockets and swallowed them whole, or when she tore up newspapers and letters before they had been read. Once she got fleas and father bought some special powder from a shop-keeper who said 'Use this and it will move all the fleas in Manchester!' We had her for fourteen years and she shared our lives, day and night, winter and summer, licked our faces and ate plates of boiled sheep's head. She knew when we were sad and when we were happy and I was certain that sometimes she could smile.

Father the Husband

Looking back over the years, I think that I was happy far more than sad. I know that I always felt secure and was fortunate in having caring parents who got on well together. I have often wondered what kind of marriage it was between my mother and father. My judgement was based, I suppose on my own needs and the level of my experience, but it also had to be assessed against the marital values of another era.

Marriage was the goal of every growing girl and simply living together was completely unacceptable. 'Living in sin' they called it. Having a child out of wedlock was a terrible disgrace which had far-reaching affects on both child and mother.

Women usually gave up work to care for husband, house and children and many simply became the docile reflections of their partner. How many talents, personal ambitions, dreams and even careers were lost in the demands of the family. These were the working women of the twenties and thirties who scrubbed floors, beat the carpets, slaved over wash tubs and conjured up meals from the cheapest foods. Nobody in the present day would recognise as edible the cow-heel, pigs trotters, scrag-end of lamb, sheep's head or tripe. Nor what it was like to visit the street markets at the end of the day when the left-over vegetables and scraps of beef could be bought cheaply.

Did those women, who juggled constantly with a shortage of shillings and pence, and sometimes went hungry themselves, ever regret their lost hopes and the expectations of young and eager brides? Lost illusions perhaps, sighs, tears or, more likely, hopeless resignation.

My own mother was proud of one thing, very unusual in those days and often boasted about it. During the marriage ceremony, she promised to love and honour my father, but the vow 'to obey' was omitted. However, in spite of her spirited stand, she did, on the whole, follow my father's wishes, if not his commands. But I know that she never completely lost the lively sparkle which father had been proud enough to marry. Once, very much later, she confided in me that she was aware of the different aspects of father.

'People see him as a wonderful man – very respected. But they don't live with him!' She may have been speaking through anger or hurt, but she said no more – ever. Nor did I.

She had, before her marriage, been Kate, the lively younger daughter of Blacksmith George's brood of children, born in the Isle of Wight, not pretty perhaps but possessing a gleam in the eye, and a lovely skin which she kept well into old age. She was a woman of strong likes and dislikes and I once listed the things which she kept as dreams (or perhaps compensations) but which rarely materialised. These included a leather coat, amber beads, pearls, pure silk, jet beads, a tailor-made suit and lilies of the valley. In the house she admired those people with ugly tiled fireplaces, red-brick doorsteps and crazy paving. She liked brass bands, Paul Robson and William Powell, the film star.

A few things on the list, after waiting for years, she eventually acquired and one in particular led to my first really serious battle with Mother. We had had babyhood fights of course, but this was different. She had, at last, replaced our two stone front-door steps (which I had to clean) with shiny brick ones. All very well, I thought, but someone is going to slip on the rounded edges. As far as I remember, no-one actually broke an ankle and mother remained proud of the silly things.

These steps, however, were not the end of the matter.

One thing led to another and what followed was, to me, a complete tragedy. It caused me many bitter tears and I think that I never, ever forgave my mother.

She had our Laburnum tree cut down!

There it had always stood, in all its glory, with long tassels of yellow blossom, the best tree in our road, and, as far as I was concerned, in the whole of Manchester. I loved it. It was my friend. But mother announced that it was in the way of the two new gate posts which she was determined to have. She wanted two ugly brick monstrosities to match the steps, with large clumsy spheres on top which, she said, were smart and very fashionable. They would be exactly the same as the others in our road.

'But our nice wooden posts are different', I protested. 'Why do we have to have the same as every body else?'

Mother grunted and looked more determined than ever.

'They'll be nice' she said, 'And very smart'.

Although she had often talked about the wretched brick gate-posts, I never thought that they would become reality. Until one Saturday morning! Two men arrived to cut down the tree, carrying large saws, sharp and threatening. I turned to mother in desperation.

'You can't cut down my lovely tree!' I cried. 'I hate those nasty fat gate-posts! There's nothing wrong with our wooden ones!'

'They've rotted', replied mother, flatly.

I shrieked, howled, begged and promised all-manner of things but nothing made the slightest difference.

I took myself off to bed, hiding my head under the blankets so that I wouldn't hear the sound of sawing, and chopping. But I could still hear the terrible creaks and rending, as the Laburnum slowly died in agony.

Mother shrugged and thought I'd taken leave of my senses. Father, although I thought he would understand, said nothing and I suddenly realised that I had over-estimated him, especially as, the following year, the Lime tree had to go too.

'It's throwing too much shadow on the front room!' he said.

I cried again but it was gone and remains only in my memory, with its light green leaves amongst which the sun shone, and its sticky flowers which attracted the bees. I knew then, that the parents whom you thought were always on your side, were often not, and from that time onwards there grew in me a certain wariness and a new certainty that life had shadows as well as sunshine.

Soon after that, there was another argument which I lost Although I said I didn't want to, my mother made me learn the piano. We had, at the time, an old mahogany instrument with a fret-worked front backed by faded silk and two brass candlesticks, one on each side. I had a teacher too. She was called Miss Louch and she had a house with a large front room in which stood, in all its glory, a shiny black grand piano. I had never seen such a splendid object and admired its white ivory keys and the black ones which made the notes sharp or flat. There was a stool with a knob on one side which you could turn in order to go up or down.

When I had learned all the notes, E G B D F and F A C E, she gave me my first music book called 'Farmyard Frolics', and father bought me a leather satchel to carry it in.

Both father and mother were quite musical. Mother possessed a good soprano voice and used to throw herself into Handel's 'Messiah' as an enthusiastic member of the church choir. I used to feel quite proud of her, up on the platform in her white blouse, her music sheet in her hand and her mouth opening wide. But my favourite times were when she sang for me. Her own best-loved song was 'What'll I do when you are far away' but she also taught me another, which originated I believe from America (because in England, little girls didn't 'holler' as they did in the song!) It went like this:

> Once there lived side by side, two little girls
> They were both dressed alike, hair down in braids,
> Blue gingham pinafores, stockings of red,
> Little sunbonnets tied on each pretty head.
> When school was over, secrets they'd tell
> Wandering hand in hand, down by the well-ell
> But one day a quarrel came, hot tears were shed
> 'I don't want to play in your yard!' But the other said
> 'You shan't play in my yard!' I don't like you any more!
> You'll be sorry when you see me swinging on our garden door
> You shan't holler down our rain barrel,
> You shan't climb our apple tree-ee
> I don't want to play in your yard if you won't be good to me'.

It is possible that I have confused the two yards and I may have mistaken some of the words, but that is how I remember it.

Father used to sing too and prided himself on his deep bass voice. I used to urge him to sing lower and lower, while mother used to laugh and say, 'You're not a patch on Paul Robson!' Father's favourite song was called 'Stars of Normandie' about a pretty girl who stood desolate on the sea-shore, waiting for her sailor-lad who had sailed away, never to return.

Mother played the piano too, totally without finesse, but with a constant use of the loud pedal and an attack on the keys which could have dislodged them all. She firmly laid down the rules for me.

'You must practise for half an hour every day. Do you hear?'

'Yes' I said, without enthusiasm.

'Lessons cost money!'

'I know'.

'We're making a sacrifice for you. Do you understand?'

'Think so'.

'Well, go along then! Scales first!'

How I hated those scales and I failed to understand what was the use of them all. Boring, useless things. And I hated the old piano and the fact that it was sun-shining outside and I was kept in like a prisoner.

One day, I hit upon a bright idea. I propped up a book on the music stand, set my fingers on automatic pilot and off I went, playing and reading at the same time. But mother was listening in the kitchen and soon became aware of an extremely odd run of scales. I looked up to see her in the doorway.

'Don't you ever do that again!' she cried, descending upon me with a furious face and I got a really hard rap on my knuckles.

'Ow' I shouted. 'That hurt!'

'Served you right' We're not paying for those lessons to have you messing about like that! Give me that book! You can have it back when I'm ready!'

So after that, I dared not try such tricks again and I said to myself, 'If ever I have a little girl, I won't make her play the piano!' The only thing I could do was to keep looking at the clock and on the dot of the half-hour, I would spring from my seat and bang down the piano lid.

'What was that banging?' mother would shout. 'You'd better watch it, young lady!'

Then I would creep to the corner where I had put my skipping rope, or whip and top, at the ready and slip outside, hoping that I wouldn't be hauled inside again, or that the cross voice would not follow me into the street.

After that, for a while, it seemed to me that mother and I were not quite so friendly as before. We seemed to have more arguments and I was always convinced that I was right. But if I lost the battle I would jump up and down behind the parlour door, pulling the most dreadful faces. If she caught me I would get a stinging slap on the legs and if I was really beyond the pale, I would be sent to bed in disgrace.

All the same, I knew that I was loved and that, in their own way, my parents were doing all this for my sake, although I often had to search my brains to find the reason why. I knew that, although she lost her temper now and again, she was a genuine and kindly lady.

Everyone else knew it too and often asked for her help. She would never refuse such a request, even though it meant leaving home sometimes, to care for a sick friend or relative, even those who were dying.

'Kate will know what to do!' 'Kate will come'. And she always did.

But sometimes she herself became ill, mainly with Bronchitis which was caused by the smog and the damp of our Northern winters. There was no talk, in those days, of the dangers of pollution and we all continued to breathe the impure air hanging like a pall over the congested areas with all their smoking chimneys. Each year, Mother would have to retire to bed, where she would lie coughing continuously. Father would light a fire in her bedroom and sometimes, if she were really bad, the doctor would be called.

Father and I used to manage the household chores between us. I was already expert at dusting, polishing and cleaning spoons, but I knew nothing about cooking. Father didn't either, so meals were 'hit and miss' affairs, with dishes either under-cooked or just caught from burning. Rice puddings were our stand-by. When mother was feeling better I would shout up the stairs.

'How many spoonfuls of rice mother? How much milk? Do I put sugar in?' Poor mother was not always left in peace.

So winters were always a challenge, and the main priority was simple – to keep warm. You sat over the fire, with your slippered feet on the fender and sometimes developed mottled legs through over-exposure to the heat. Warm at the front, there was always a chill at the back. No central heating in those days, or double-glazing. If you were lucky, you had a square of carpet on the lino. It was agony going upstairs to your bedroom on a freezing night, when the patterns of frost on the windows made the outside world invisible. When I went to school on a chilly morning, when snow dusted the trees and ice made the pavements slippery, Mother always put my coat, gloves and scarf in front of the fire. Hopefully I remained snug and warm until I reached school. And I knew that mother had been up an hour before father and me, in order to rake the ashes and to light that fire. She always made porridge in winter for my breakfast.

'Warm clothes and nice hot porridge inside you ! You'll come to no harm', she would say.

One morning, at breakfast mother suddenly said 'When I was kneeling in front of the grate I smelled that scent of flowers. That's the second time!' I was fascinated and firmly believed, as she did I think, that the perfume related to some ghostly presence.

Winter fires! People who have never experienced the blaze from a coal fire, in a black polished grate, have missed a great deal. True, they have escaped the smoke and the dust, but neither have they known the dancing flames which curled round the shiny pieces of coal and then escaped up the chimney. Nor have they seen the flickering shadows on the kitchen walls.

A warm fire, a warm home, in the midst of a chilly world!

Chapter 7

High School Days and Holidays

WHEN I WAS TEN, going on eleven, it was the scholarship year when children sat for an examination which gained entrance into various types of school, and gaining a scholarship signified a certain amount of prestige. Miss McMinn redoubled her efforts, marking us slave over arithmetical problems (no calculators in those days), do mental sums in pounds, shillings and pence and write compositions. She had, I think, a reputation to keep, that of having the most pupils gain placed in a grammar school. No doubt I owed a great deal to Miss McMinn, for I gained admission to Manchester High School. A genuine 'super – teacher' she was!

When September came, I was prepared for my new adventure, not realising that it would completely change my life. The rather anxious child who entered the system was not the same girl who eventually left it, having been pushed, pressured and polished like everyone else. There was one problem. Although my parents never said anything directly to me, they did not find it easy when new financial demands were forced upon them and more sacrifices had to be made. Each term there were new books to buy, uniform to provide, (according to a list of instructions and purchased from chosen shops). There were black gym – slips, white blouses, black stockings or white socks for summer, plimsolls for P.T. and a pair of indoor shoes into which we all had to change every day. We had a black velour hat for winter (with elastic under the chin), and a straw one for summer, both with a yellow and black band. And gloves had to be worn.

After Easter the whole school was curiously rejuvenated as we cast off our black hats and gym-slips, replacing them with cotton checked dresses and the straw hats. It made a nice change as we poured into school on the first day of the summer term – a chattering mob, hats bobbing, until the sound of a bell turned us all back into subdued automatons.

There seemed to be a distinct division between winter and summer and, like the trees and plants, we felt the sap rising! New freedoms, more air and sunshine and, so with lighter steps, we skipped happily into spring. Sometimes the weather turned hot in May and I begged to be allowed to cast my liberty – bodice and warm skirt.

'Not yet,' mother used to say, 'Never cast a clout till May is out.' I thought that was quite a stupid instruction because summer had often begun.

But the school building, which contained very little sun and air, was old and as a new-comer it seemed to me over poweringly enormous. There were three floors including the attics, where the art rooms and the biology lab were situated. There was a dusty, strange basement where the boilers and heating pipes were and one huge playroom which was used in breaks and dinner hours. There were many staircases to climb and movement to and from classes were strictly controlled and made in total silence, except for the pattering of those indoor shoes. I often got a disorder mark for chattering (unobserved as I thought), when I had not noticed a lurking prefect.

Here and there, in the corridors, were life sized statues of Greek goddesses which looked totally out of place and were ignored by all. The only statue which we found interesting was in the art room because he was a handsome male figure and wore a fig – leaf.

The girls in my form (no longer a 'class'), were an affable crowd and we more or less stayed together all through our school years. One became a special friend and our friendship has lasted far beyond our school days. In deed we still meet, we laugh and we remember, even now. She was called Ena, the name being inspired by, I believe, Queen Ena of Spain.

Many of the girls were fee-paying and we soon found that there was an indefinable but distinct difference between them and we scholarship girls. For a start, they could all afford school dinners (home made sandwiches for us!), and they all seemed to live in big houses. Their fathers had cars. They were in different forms from us because (we told ourselves), they were not so advanced and did cookery instead of science. This gave us, (I suppose), some sort of compensation, but if we called them snobs, what were we with our scholastic pretensions!

Our Head mistress had, it seemed, a set of double standards. On the one hand she depended on us to gain the best results in exams and to reach the colleges and Universities. On the other hand, she courted the non-academics and the well-to-do, the daughters of solicitors, doctors or successful businessmen. She promoted their social graces and insisted that we all became identical, glove-wearing, hat-adorned pupils who were told to be proud of our school and its historical inheritance. The truth about uniforms, was of course, that they reduced everyone to one common denominator and, glancing at the innocent schoolgirl one could not tell whether her father was the local undertaker, the coal merchant or the hospital surgeon. In the great hall, where we met for school assembly every morning, were enormous shiny black panels mounted on the walls, so that we could admire and maybe aspire to, the achievements of former girls, their names and dates in gleaming gold lettering. (Who *was* that Amelia Gertrude Wells 1908-1914!).

We had a vague connection with Manchester Grammar School for Boys, but it remained theoretical and we knew them only as boys in blue-ringed caps who passed us in the streets or occasionally rode on trams. In our Senior Years we used to think how impossibly exciting it would be if they were invited to our Sixth-form Dances. But no! Boys were never part of the stilted affairs, when girls danced with girls, when we dressed to out-vie each other and practised our grown-up airs (thank goodness my mother was a dressmaker!) It was always quite fascinating, however, to have a glimpse of what we might one day become, with our adult hairstyles, a mere suggestion of make-up and our careful deportment learned form the Gym Mistress. (My nose was powdered in the cloakroom, because father said that make-up was the sign of a wicked woman). A few girls looked quite dazzling and I remember one time when my Special Friend became a dusky beauty with her dark skin, brown eyes and a beautiful peach dress. Only in the cloakroom did we return to being school-girls with our chatterings and gigglings and our dreams of boys who were never there. The days of a co-education were not yet.

Once, however, a young man did try to scale the ramparts and gain admission. He never succeeded. It was Manchester University Rag Day when the students, dressed in fancy costume, went around with rattling tins, collecting money for the local hospitals. They also sold their Rag Magazine which we were not supposed to read because it contained some rude bits. My Special Friend and I were in charge of the Fiction Library, the windows of which overlooked the street and the school entrance. Suddenly we heard a voice, quite decidedly masculine, shouting in the street below. Excitedly and suitably intrigued, we threw up the sash window and leaned out.

'Want to buy our magazine?' Said the Voice.

'Love to, but we've no money,' I said.

'A pity. Well, do you think I can come in?'

'Not very likely' we replied. 'It's a Nunnery, but of course you can try!'

'Oh', he laughed. 'Sorry! I thought it was a school for young ladies.

By this time we were halfway out of the window, exhibiting to anyone who entered the room the spectacle of two pairs of black stockings and black knickers with a half-moon of pink flesh on display.

'What do you think you're doing!' cried an angry voice. 'Shut that window at once! You'll be reported for this!' Did teachers **never** understand?

I suppose that we were reported, but maybe they were more understanding than we thought, for I can't remember any punishment.

Thus, completely alien to much of our present-day culture (except perhaps at the summit of the social scale), this double emphasis on academic progress and a type of social polish, was very much a feature of our High School days. Nothing was actually stated but certain rules were there to follow, so that we absorbed a kind of second-hand gentility, with the wearing of gloves, no eating in the streets, seats given up to our elders and voices kept low and lady-like. We had to say 'Perspiration' and never

'Sweat'. Any deviation from the norm would have been shocking but I can't remember that anyone actually digressed. As far as I know, nobody smoked and I think that no-one knew a real swear-word, let alone used it.

Accents were smoothed out and some of us, falling miserably short, were propelled willy-nilly into the extra-curricular Elocution Class. I was one and I felt sorry that it was apparently necessary for my parents to pay for the privilege. I must have made some progress (since my Harry Hoggart days!) because I was called upon to recite a piece out of 'Hiawatha' in a Speech Competition. My parents had Lancashire accents and so what actually happened was probably inevitable. I developed two different levels, as it were – my posh voice at school and my plainer one at home. I don't think that any of this was of real help because I also developed some confusion. I realised that suddenly I was finding it difficult to accept the 'summat' (for something) and 'owt' (for anything) which my mother often used.

It was no wonder that Mrs. Owen and her family, next door, were known to call me a little snob.

Our teachers also had to be the best. They were all graduates of Girton and the like, and, as always, they mere unmarried and mostly middle-aged, although, for a short time, there arrived a young teacher of Greek. She was possibly in her twenties but was soon set in the same mould as all the others, hair scraped back in a bun, horn-rimmed glasses and a serious expression. Was it not acceptable to be pretty as well as brainy, I pondered, or at least end up with some sort of compromise?

We knew nothing of their lives, where they resided or whether the aura of 'teacher' ever deserted them. I think not. We felt that it was a real discovery if someone found out a Christian name and how incongruously it sat upon the 'Miss' whom we knew in school. Nick-names were a mark of affection and rarely did any teacher have this honour. One member of staff, however, did have a romantic past, although I have no idea how it was discovered. She was reputed to have lost her fiancé in the First World War and her heart had broken, they said. She had white hair which had been caused by the shock (we were told – by 'someone who knew') and so she was destined to remain unmarried because she wouldn't have a second chance.

The rest of the teaching staff was judged by us in various categories. They were boring, frightening, hard or soft and only the odd one or two were deemed to be likeable or even remotely interested in their pupils. Praise seemed to be in short supply and competition encouraged. But eccentrics abounded. There was the Latin Teacher to whom we had to say 'Salve O Magistra' and who broke into wide grins for no apparent reason. Puzzling really, when all we had to read about were boring old Roman farmers. Then there was one hated Maths Teacher who always seemed to know when I had reached the perplexing bit. She would haul me out in front of the blackboard to solve an Algebraic equation and poured scorn upon me when I couldn't. She made me hate Maths.

The Gymnastics teacher we all thought too old for the job because she had faded hair and wrinkles. She certainly did not fit into the stereotype of a Games Mistress in our stories about 'Morcove' or 'Miss Cherry of Saint Gabriels'. At the end of each lesson we had to thank her with a sideways step, a heel click and a chorused 'Thank you Miss Bourne'. I always objected to her insistence that we must stand in a file in order of height. Of course I didn't like it because I was always second from the front!

Physics and Chemistry teachers I could not abide because I associated them with the smell of the Labs with their odour of pungent gas and Bunsen burners.

The Biology Teacher fared better, in my opinion, and my Special Friend and I had many adventures under her supervision. Like cutting up an Ox's eye, or a worm. Special Friend said she felt sick when she saw the eye and I said that it was a good job she wasn't an Arab because they used to eat them for dinner. Anyway, I cut open her specimen as well as my own and expressed horror at the sticky jelly which ran out.

The room itself was high under a sloping roof with fascinating exhibits on tables and shelves. One of our favourites was an Axelotle, with its black velvety coat, living in a tank. There was always a collection of Stick Insects and once I was persuaded to take one home in a jar. I couldn't get fond of it and Mother threatened to put it in the dustbin. I can't remember what happened to it.

There were bottles of brains, pickled in formaldehyde, diagrams of frogs insides, drawers full of knives and scalpels and wonderful microscopes. When we had nothing better to do, we examined pieces of nail, a red hair, some spit and a prick of blood. We tested some drinking water to see what they gave us in the cloakroom taps and we found a creature in it with several pairs of legs. Best of all, there was a real skeleton in one corner, usually draped with a cloth, but when he wasn't, I caught him grinning at me more than once. So fascinating did I find him that we invented 'The Skeleton Pictorial' describing snippets of skeletal 'goings-on' – like weddings (no funerals of course) bone-rattling competitions, Groaning Festivals and so on. I still have the one-and-only edition and I have the feeling that it must be unique!

At the opposite end of the scale there was that one subject which left me cold. That was Latin (in spite of the affable teacher with her sporadic grins) So I decided that it was a complete waste of time (and I had already spent three years on it!) I thought that Spanish would be a better alternative for, after all, it was based on Latin, wasn't it! But, coward that I was, I sent my Father to face Miss Clarke, the Headmistress, in her den.

'Tell her I refuse to do Latin' I said.

Father smiled rather bleakly.

'Much better to be positive. I'll just say that you are really keen to do Spanish.

'And that you quite agree', I urged.

I knew that Father was not looking forward to meeting Miss Clarke because she was on her own ground, he said, and that would be to her advantage. But he went, we won the day and the next term Best Friend and I were learning Spanish, just a handful of us in a tiny class. Much better than Latin!

I felt rather triumphant that we had won a round against the formidable Miss Clarke, but in retrospect, it was quite probable that she didn't consider that I was worthy enough material to even pursue the argument. She got her own back too! At the end of one of my Senior form reports, she had written 'Annie is a slow developer!'

Many years later, best friend and I saw Miss Clarke again, and without her authority, sitting in a Shropshire hotel.

'Oh my god!' I said, 'I've forgotten my school hat!'

*   *   *

School did not, of course, take over my whole existence. Life went on outside! After lessons were over and homework finished, there were remnants of evenings and weekends when I used to wake up and say 'Oh good! It's Saturday!' There were long holidays throughout the school year.

The activities of my early years centred round the areas where I lived, but as I grew older, I went further afield and often into the great city itself, sometimes with mother and sometimes alone or with a friend. Nowadays it is perhaps difficult to understand that children could journey alone into busy areas and that even the side streets presented no threat. By the time

Taken in 1906, Manchester as it was.

I was twelve or thirteen, I knew all the highways and by-ways of the city, with short-cuts to anywhere.

The only danger in the children's playground was if you fell to the ground from a swing and cut your knees on the sharp grit! I am not sure if my parents ever worried about my solitary excursions, but they did lay down rules and the time I was expected to be home.

Manchester was an exciting place, especially to one who could not get enough of the bustle and vitality of the city life. It was the centre of commerce and cotton industry and its enormous warehouses of blackened stone and a multitude of windows were linked by cobbled streets. Here and there a canal showed itself among the buildings, dark grey water half hidden by bridges and even darker shadows.

There were three great stations with converging train lines and signal boxes and enormous monsters of smoking engines under glass roofing, too black to see the sky. City squares were vivid with stores, teeming with people and traffic. Great dray horses pulled carts with huge bales of cotton, smart little ponies, high-stepping, trotted easily with their traps labelled 'The Manchester Guardian' and 'Evening News'. Pedlars stood at pavement edgings with trays of jumping beans, baubles and balloons, all for a penny or less. At one corner there was always a poor man, pale and bearded, seated on a wooden board with wheels. He sold matches and his cap was on the pavement beside him. He had no legs for he was one of the legions of the wounded from World War One which I had been told about but could not begin to imagine.

I knew of a secret square where people could sit, doing no more than watching the pigeons and the city sparrows. Shafts of pale sunshine, all that the sun could spare, slanted between the buildings to the benches where people sat – old men in cloth caps and mufflers, office workers with blank expressions on grey city faces. The sounds of the traffic were far away as a tramp gloated over the discovery of a fag or a half-eaten sandwich.

Close by, were the old streets with old names. Old Millgate, Market Street, Deansgate and Hanging Ditch. Shudehill was alive with traders selling their wares, fish, fruit and puppy dogs. Books for a few pence, dusty from the city grime. A grey lady selling golden daffodils.

Mother and I always went to town on Divi Day. This was because she had collected small tickets each time she had shopped at the local Co-op and I had played my part by sticking them on to a sheet of paper. Each had a number which I still remember – 1,7,9,3,2. The sheet of tickets was then exchanged for money, two notes perhaps, which were put carefully into her black purse. Then we would go shopping – into Woolworth's, where nothing cost more than sixpence, or Marks and Spencer's, a modest shop where everything was cheap. Some stores on Deansgate we avoided because you had to be very rich to shop there. But usually we could afford waffles in Lewis' basement – crispy battered slices with a tiny jug of sticky golden syrup.

During my High school days, summer holidays stretched wonderfully from mid-July until mid-September, bright with promise. I was never bored nor did I ever get tired of my own company, for the world was out there for my discovery. On my first day I always walked to the public library, dimly lit, a storehouse of books all waiting patiently to be borrowed.

Silence was the rule, and the only sound was that of the rubber stamp gently thumping the date onto a chosen book, and if you had to speak, it had to be a whisper. My earliest favourite book was 'Wind in the Willows' and I liked 'What Katie Did' and 'Princess and the Goblin', but I never admired 'Alice in Wonderland', which struck me as callous and rather cruel. Poetry I loved and I had my own collection, reading and learning it when I was supposed to be asleep in bed. But I read under the bedclothes with a torch, no doubt increasing my short sight.

Parks were fun too, with little paths which often led to nowhere, and bushes where a child could live in a fantasy world and be perfectly safe. The trees were too tall to climb and it was forbidden anyway by a rather cross-looking park keeper in uniform. There was a fountain where I could squirt water into my mouth and a small fenced – off area curtaining a large black stone which, they said, was a piece of meteor which had dropped from the sky.

Sometimes, indeed quite often, I went to the swimming baths and when my cousin Bessie came to stay, she always went with me. We taught ourselves to swim and spent many hours in the blue, bitter tasting water.

'I like swimming under water best' I said.

'You're like a fish', someone said.

'I am a fish!' I replied.

At about this time, a carpenter friend of ours made me my own swing in the garden. Happy, carefree days! I thought that there couldn't be anything better than soaring up towards the sky and down again, because my imagination took me for beyond our back garden.

Rainy days! Somehow I remember very few. But I never minded staying indoors. Sometimes, at five o'clock, I clamped little ear-phones on my head and I listened to Children's' Hour, with its Uncle Eric and Auntie Muriel, Romany and a rather stupid Toy Town with Dennis the Dachshund and Larry the Lamb. But occasionally mother would spoil things by announcing that it was time to clean the cutlery.

'Well now', she would say. 'As you can't go out, you might as well help me with the spoons and the brass candlesticks! Put your pinny on, first'.

It was a job that I was definitely not fond of and I hated the smell of Brasso.

'I don't mind going out in the rain', I said hopefully.

It was no use. The spoons and the forks and the candlesticks were already set out on newspaper on the kitchen table. 'Get on with it!' Mother said.

It was true that I liked rain, clad in raincoat sou-wester and black shiny wellingtons. Puddles were there to be splashed in and to reflect the silver of the sky. I liked the wind even better. If it was really strong, late at night,

I used to listen to its blustering, as I lay in a warm bed. I was, after all, born in windy March.

My parents could afford very few holidays, but for one week in August we had a short stay in the fishing port of Fleetwood or in North Wales and for that, mother and father had saved up all year. Often we went with an aunt and uncle, with cousins who were company for me. Boarding houses were usual and the sea-side towns produced a myriad of land-ladies who let their rooms for a modest fee. Provisions for breakfast and high tea were brought in by the visitors, for the land-lady to cook. An odd arrangement but it seemed to solve any problem of making those ends meet!

We kids did all the usual things, building sand-castles with moats that a spoil-sport always jumped on 'Aw! Look what you've done! That's not fair!'

And a handful of sand whizzed in his direction. We splashed in the waves, tried not to tread on the jelly-fish and buried Father in the sand, while the sandwiches got full of grit and the lemonade was warm. Father used to sit on a rented deck-chair without his jacket, wearing a white handkerchief on his head, knotted at each corner. He used to go very pink. Beaches were not like those of today, when people, already brown, lie like herrings and try to get browner still. There was, however, a complete ignorance about the dangerous effects of sunshine and whenever the temperature rose, fair-skinned and freckled as I was, my arms and back went a feverish red and the next day peeled off in ribbons. Sometimes it burned and I cried. Mother smothered me in Calamine lotion.

One year we went to the outdoor swimming pool, my cousin Frank and I. Mother had knitted a bathing costume for me, so I proudly pulled it on, with its blue and white stripes. Then I ran to the edge of the pool, dipped down into the water and stood up again. To my horror, my costume had slipped down to my knees.

'Heck!' said cousin Frank.

I fled to Mother. 'You've made it too big!' I cried. 'It will fit Auntie Janie!'

'I followed the pattern', said Mother flatly. 'The wool's stretched, that's all!'

Well it would, wouldn't it, I thought.

*   *   *

The greatest distance I travelled in those days was to the Isle of Wight, where we had some second cousins. It was a long and exciting journey which entailed getting up at the crack of dawn and catching two trains. There were five of us, myself, my mother and father and two cousins, Winnie and Edna. My memories are rather vague but I remember constant southern sunshine (somehow different from our Lancashire variety) and I have a recollection of playing with a whole lot of second-cousins in the large garden of a house in Ryde. I knew that Grand-dad George had lived in Ryde before he moved up North, and my mother had been born there.

But one particular day I do recall – when we visited an old relative who lived in one of the smallest cottages I had ever seen. It was all kitchen and not much else. The toilet was another of the bottom-of-the-garden variety, with a hole in a plank and it smelled so awful that I tried not to breathe as I sat there.

In the kitchen was an enormous table, made of cleanly scrubbed wood and set with five thick white plates and five mugs of very strong tea. In the centre was a baking bowl filled with lettuce leaves and a mound of thickly-sliced bread and butter.

'Sit down and help yourselves', said our hostess. I sat down and looked round for something else to eat and I was just going to whisper to Mother, 'Is there anything else?' when she silenced me with a warning frown. The old lady did not eat. She sat in her rocking chair, smiling affably while we wondered how to begin.

'Help yourselves!' she said.

We ploughed our way through the hunks of bread and the lettuce leaves which we ate with our fingers. I thought longingly of Mother's Hot Pot. All this seemed to eliminate any conversation and silence prevailed in the kitchen, apart from the crunching of lettuce and the buzz of a few blue bottles in the window. One of my cousins had a distinct twinkle in the eye and was turning bright pink. I dared not catch her glance.

The old lady said nothing and continued to smile. I wondered if she was very poor, or if she was, in her own way, giving us a treat.

Once more she said, 'Help ourselves! There's plenty more lettuce in the garden!'

A spluttering cough from me was silenced by my Mother's baleful eye!

But on the walk back, like children who were let out of school, we happily sang a song of our own invention

> There's plenty more lettuce
> In the garden
> There's plenty more lettuce
> In the garden! Help yourselves!

And even Mother smiled and did not forbid it!

Chapter 8

Teen Years

Y TEENS CREPT upon me stealthily but I felt no difference for, in contrast to the present day, maturity came more slowly and we seemed to remain children much longer. My life followed a predictable pattern – lessons, homework, and exams at one end of the scale and times of leisure at the other, which were treasured and spent according to whim.

School continued its routine and never varied. I caught the 8.20 tram every morning, at the top of our road, was never late and was home again at 4.15. The same girls who entered school at eleven, were still there when they reached eighteen. Teachers had presumably reached the middle of a gratifying career and stayed. We sat every July in regimented rows on Speech Day and some of us won prizes which we had to accept with a curtsey. We breathed in the solemnity of Founders Day and thanked God for those who had established our school and all who had served therein.

In summer and winter we all plied to and fro, unquestioning and dutiful. Only foggy days disturbed the pattern, when gradually during the day a great yellow pall crept over the City. Sounds became muffled, even the birds ceased their twittering and eventually the traffic stopped, unable to continue blindly in the blanketed streets. To our delight, we were sent home early, to find a tram which, if we were lucky, would emerge eerily from the greyness. Failing that, we had to walk, somehow managing to find our way home, a distance of three miles or so. We tripped over pavement edges. Eyes stinging, we looked for anything familiar, hands plunged in pockets and huddled in scarves damp with freezing fog. Meeting anyone was a ghostly encounter when a hazy figure would loom into view and then disappear again into the void. The fog had a rank murkiness which seeped into lungs, so that people with Bronchitis suffered badly, including my poor mother.

Thus the thirties were upon us. In my own small world it seemed that life was taking a turn for the better. Now we had talking films – the wonderful Broadway spectacles and one of the first 'tear-jerkers' which had given us Al Jolson singing 'Sonny Boy' so that no-one left the cinema with dry eyes.

Father once took me to see 'The Midsummer Night's Dream' at the Opera House, a dazzling theatre where we sat in the 'Gods' for a shilling.

Skirts had grown longer and I had my first bra and a pair of higher heels on square-toed shoes. The first edition of 'Woman' and 'Womans's Own' appeared. Mr. Smith the dentist, began to give injections for my fillings!

In the wider world, the decade began with a tragedy when a British airship R101 crashed on its first flight. Like the Titanic it should never have happened. Then, one day, in 1936, a new shock was in store. Boys were in town selling newspapers with a screaming headline 'Abdication of Edward VIII'. He was determined to marry his Mrs. Simpson and had to give up being King. The whole of England seemed stunned and the papers said that we were part of history, and that nothing would be the same again. 'Well, it never is, is it?' I thought. 'You can't turn the clock back', said mother in one of her wiser moments.

In the wider world, history was even more tragic and people began to talk of a Depression. There was mass unemployment and pawn shops were kept busy from Monday to Friday. It was known as going to Uncles! Miners were desperate and workers from the ship-yards were marching to London. None of this actually affected us or anyone I knew but I was aware of it like a shadow in the background because all was not well. My father declared that he was a Liberal and waged a verbal war against all the titled and rich landowners who, he protested, had no right to hold on to all those acres of land which could have been allotted to poorer folk. He wanted the Land Laws changed, whatever that meant.

At home, Mother decided that we needed more income ourselves, and so, in order to 'make ends meet' (as she always put it) she expressed her intention of taking in a lodger.

'We don't know anybody', said father.

'Yes, we do. I saw Alice the other day and she needs somewhere to live. I thought that we could let her have Annie's bedroom and she can eat her meals with us'.

I wasn't sure if I agreed with all that, but was suitably appeased when mother said that she would make the tiny third bedroom pretty for me.

'We'll buy some green material from the market and make you a corner wardrobe with a shelf. And I'm sure we can manage a dressing table.'

And so she did! Out of two orange boxes. So I was quite happy there and I could still see the garden and the trains.

Then one day, Alice arrived. She was an unmarried friend of my mother's – a smartly-dressed, pleasant lady who, however, was not given to divulging her inner thoughts or anything concerning her daily life. But we knew that she worked behind the counter in the Post Office, a situation that my mother admired because Alice would end up with a comfortable pension, (and so she did, I believe). She came and went quickly, politely ate her meals without comment and we hardly knew she was there.

On the dressing-table in her bedroom, she kept an astonishing array of scent bottles, lotions, powders and brushes at which I often peeped but never touched – as secretive as she was. She must have been in her early forties, neat and slim but her hair was crimped and curled to death, so that it had lost any lustre which once it had.

Two happenings concerned Alice. One evening, my father came home with the astonishing news that he had, quite positively, seen her sitting with a man, in a car parked in a nearby road.

'Never!' exclaimed mother.

'It was her all right!' replied father.

'Did you raise your hat and say 'Good evening, Alice!' I enquired earnestly.

'Of course not! She never saw me!'

I had a vision of father in his trilby hat, coat collar turned up, sneaking sidelong glances past Alice and her mystery man.

'Father the detective!' I said to myself and then, less kindly, father the spy. I was thinking of those films in black and white where the detective always got his man and his girl-friend spoke in stilted language as if (Mother said) 'she had a plum in her mouth'.

Anyway it was all very interesting and it gave Alice a new aura, especially as there was something very odd about it all, as if the man was brought out secretly only at night, never to be seen in the light of day. 'I can't imagine her kissing him!' I thought. 'But then you never know'.

'Perhaps she will decide to fetch him out of the car and bring him to see us', I suggested.

'Not likely!' said mother. 'Always a dark horse that one! She once had a fiancé who died and left her all his money. He was called Jack'.

'He couldn't have been very old'. I said. 'What did he die of?' – ever eager to know the details.

'How should I know! But his family were very put out. She shouldn't have kept it, they said'.

'So is she rich?'

'Quite well off I suppose'.

I thought about this. 'She doesn't look rich' I said. 'Has she spent it all, do you think?'

'Not her! It will be salted away in the post Office – every penny!'

'She has got some lovely rings and a gold watch' I remembered.

'Well there we are then!' said mother, her way of concluding the conversation.

But some weeks later, another chapter was added to the story of Alice. One summer evening when none of us was at home (I can't remember where the dog was) we had burglars. We found the scullery window broken where they had pushed the catch and climbed in. Father went out to the phone box and soon a real-life policeman came on his bike, bringing with him an exciting air of authority. Policemen had to be six feet tall in those days and he seemed to fill the kitchen. I had never been so close to a man of law before this and was intrigued by the silver buttons and all the pockets. He took off his tall helmet and pulled out a little black notebook.

'It is obvious what they did' he announced. 'They waited until a train was passing and then they shattered the glass. No-one would hear.'

Then the Policeman tramped upstairs, followed by the three of us, plus the dog.

'Ah!' he said as he found that the only room which had evidence of disturbance was that belonging to Alice.

'The window's open! See!'

He leaned outside. 'There's some footprints on the grass. Somebody jumped out!'

'But he would break a leg!' I said, concerned.

'Ssh Annie! He's thinking!'

'Probably a young lad' he pronounced. 'Now, whose bedroom is this?'

'It used to be mine' I chipped in. 'But now it belongs to Alice. She's our lodger'.

Mother glared. 'Be quiet, I said!'

'Right! We shall need a statement from Alice. Any idea where she is?'

'She's out!' I interrupted again.

I didn't know why mother didn't want me to speak because the Policeman obviously appreciated my assistance.

At that moment we heard the front door opening. I ran to the landing and peered down.

'She's here!' I announced.

Alice came up quietly, unsuspecting, and found all of us in her bedroom. She looked quite horrified.

'We've been burgled!' I exclaimed, in great excitement.

Alice took it all fairly calmly, in her usual tight-lipped manner. She found, however, that two rings and a gold brooch were missing.

'Are you insured?' asked father, always practical. She wasn't and the jewellery was never recovered.

The Policeman asked some more questions, then fastened his little book with a piece of elastic, picked up his helmet and departed on his bicycle.

'Well!' said mother, after we were back downstairs. 'Good job they didn't find anything of ours worth taking!' Of course in those days, there was less to steal – no televisions or tape recorders and they had evidently not been interested in Alice's wind-up gramophone or the records of 'Desert Song', Gallicurci the Soprano and Caruso.

But a thought struck, me and I hurried back upstairs into my own little bedroom, to see if any of my treasures had been stolen. But no. My green glass vase with a chip in it, the pair of pottery shoes, and my glass tower from Blackpool containing coloured sand, all remained as I had left them.

'That's all right then', I thought.

I rather enjoyed the fame which followed because ours was the only house which had been burgled.

Eventually Alice left us and went to live in her own flat which was notable for having 20 cushions on her three-piece suite.

*   *   *

Six months later, Auntie Kate came to live with us. She paid my mother 'for her keep', a modest sum I believe, because my parents knew that she had nowhere to live and offered to give her a home. She came from a fascinating family and was the sister of that forbidding Lizzie who had given me a threepenny bit for sitting still on a buffet. There had been six children in Kate and Lizzie's family and their grand-father was old Mr. Brown who was my Father's Uncle. As a boy, my father used to accompany him to the Wesleyan Chapel but when he could no longer walk easily, he spent his days in a fire-side chair, pondering on many things. He used to say that, one day, we would all be able to sit in our homes with a wooden box through which would come the sound of chapel hymns and the Preacher's voice. This was probably about 1898, before the radio was put into general use.

As their mother was a semi-invalid for many years, the family relied for its survival upon the four daughters who ran the household. As well as Lizzie and Kate, there were Jane and Jenny. Jane was the adventurous one and Jenny the pretty one who, it was whispered, had given birth to a son and had to find a husband to marry rather quickly. She found a hunch-backed gentleman with a handsome face and pleasant manner and it was put about that he was all she could expect in the circumstances. It was a little later that I came to know Jenny and I really liked her. I was always pleased when she came on a visit to have mother's special tea, boiled egg and bread and butter. I remained puzzled by all the whispery gossip and understood even less when mother said to father, 'Well! She could never say 'No''

The eldest sister Jane was the one who brought the real excitement to the family. Trained as a nurse, she had set off on board ship for Australia. She never reached it, for while the ship was docked near the Greek mainland, she heard of an invalid lady who was in need of care. Jane left the boat and stayed until the old lady died, leaving Jane a large sum of money. She returned to England, but did not have long to enjoy it, for she herself became ill and died.

Her money was divided between a brother and the three sisters who each received six hundred pounds, 'a tidy sum', as my mother said. There was also an amount of jewellery, including some beautiful opals, the idea of which fascinated me for years.

It seemed to me that the money did not bring any happiness. Fierce Lizzie put hers in the Bank and was too mean to spend a penny. She continued to live in the large old house which I had visited. Jenny's share was soon spent (probably, I thought, because she still couldn't say 'No') She now had two sons but nowhere to live, so she and her husband moved in with Lizzie, who treated them shabbily. They had to use the kitchen and were never allowed into that fancy parlour. Her husband and one son called Bert, mended boots for a living and mending boots meant using the cellar. 'No room up here!' she said.

So they worked all day down a steep flight of steps in that damp cellar of Lizzie's big house. It was like a prison, with a cold flagged floor, brick walls running with damp and a tiny window which allowed in very little light. I went down there only once and soon came up again, wrinkling my nose in distaste. 'It's like it was a hundred years ago!' said mother.

After a year or two, Bert (the youngest son), became ill with a racking cough which never improved, and sadly he died with tuberculosis.

'No wonder!' said my mother. 'He shouldn't have been working in all that cold and damp!'

'And all that leather!' she added. 'You never know what's in leather'

I made a mental note to breathe the freshest air I could find and never to stay in a damp cellar. But it wasn't too easy in winter with all that fog!

Cousin Kate came to live with us when I was fourteen for she had nowhere else to go. She was different from the bossy Lizzie and from the quiet defenceless Jenny. She was small and fat, with a hoisted up bosom like a pouter pigeon. She wore dark dresses, buttoned up to the neck and down to the ankles. I knew what she wore underneath! A pair of enormous dark knickers with legs to the knees – because I used to see them on the washing line.

She had put her money in the bank, advised by father and she paid my mother enough to cover her food and lodging. One day, I came home from school to find a wonderful thing – a splendid new piano, with two brass pedals and the name 'Broadwood' written in gold on the lid. I could hardly believe it, and I stood there, just staring.

'Whose is it?' I asked.

'It's ours!' said mother proudly, 'From Auntie Kate'.

The ivory keys shone and it sounded quite wonderful. I decided that on such an instrument it might be worth trying my best and from that time on, I did. One thing spoiled it however, and it was my first experience of people's envy. Auntie Kate's relatives keeping an eye on her money, no doubt, declared that she had been 'got round' and should not have bought it. My parents were incensed and upset, for nothing was further from the truth, and it caused what my mother called 'family bother'.

Kate, like Lizzie, had never married and it seemed to me (after giving it considerable thought), that she had a blank space inside her which had never been filled. So one day, she fell in love with God.

It also happened that, not far from where we lived, was a kind of church – a Tabernacle called Bethshan, where people gathered under the watchful eye of a Pastor. Kate forsook the Weslyan chapel (now called Methodist), where she used to go with mother, and became a weekly visitor at Bethshan, being much attracted to the enthusiastic singing, the frantic waving of arms and the feverish voice of the preacher. She became more and more impressed as people began to march to the front of the hall, and to declare themselves 'saved'. Having been duly saved, herself, she returned home with ecstatic gaze, clutching a bible to her bosom. None of us knew what to do, especially as she declared that she had donated a generous sum of money to the preacher.

'Doesn't seem right,' pronounced father.

'All they want is her money,' added mother.

I piped up with an idea of my own,

'Do you think they know that she's got six hundred pounds in the bank?' I asked.

'What did you say?' asked father.

'She has six hundred pounds in the bank,' I repeated.

'Well, a bit less now because she's given some away and bought ——.'
Mother cut me short.

'Don't let anyone hear you say that! We don't want it known all round Manchester! Do you hear?'

'Yes,' I muttered, wondering what she would say if she found out that I had confided everything to my best friend.

Auntie Kate burst into song, something about an old rugged cross, which, at the time, I had not heard of. Mother tried to persuade her into fewer visits to Bethshan, but off she would go, to keep her appointment with God.

One night, when we had all gone to bed, mother woke and saw a light in the bathroom, and heard the sound of running water. Kate was there, in her flannel night-dress, washing her bible, then drying it with a towel, all damp and soggy, with the pages stuck together.

'We must take her to the doctor,' said mother, the next day, and I couldn't wait to get to school so that I could relay the new exciting instalment to my best friend. With instructions not to tell! We decided, after much consideration, that, in common parlance, Auntie Kate had 'gone off her rocker'.

'Maybe she'll have to go to one of those hospitals where they take crazy people who don't know what they're talking about!'

'Well ——,' said my best friend, and then the bell went.

Kate was duly taken to the doctor who gave her some pills to take, to keep her calm, but they seemed to have little effect, as we discovered one morning. She gave my mother the shock of her life, and as I came down to breakfast I saw that my parents were both gazing in horrified silence at Auntie Kate.

She had cut off her long grey hair, usually worn in a bun, and her head was now covered with a prickly, uneven stubble. The hair was lying in an abandoned heap on the floor, along with the kitchen scissors.

'Oh Auntie Kate!' I said, 'You've cut all your hair off!'

Mother was jolted into action.

'Have your breakfast Annie,' she said, 'And get yourself off to school. I'll try to make Auntie Kate look a bit better.'

'Well,' I said. 'She shouldn't have used the kitchen scissors. They're blunt!'

Father interrupted. 'Breakfast! Come on!'

At school that day, I didn't know what to think.

'Do you think it's funny?' I asked best friend.

'Not really,' she said.

I have no recollection of the details which followed, but it seemed that the worst was over. My parents and especially my mother, showed great patience and kindness and never referred again to those recent events. Gradually, Kate returned to normal. Bethshan Tabernacle was abandoned and mother took her back to the Methodist church where they both sang happily in the choir. Kate began to chuckle again, as she used to do.

Soon, the whole episode seemed forgotten, except by me. And the hair soon grew again.

Chapter 9

Through the Eyes of a Child

I N WRITING a life story, we are inevitably aware of TIME, which appears divided and unconnected, yet is a whole continuous thread.

The early events of my own life were clearly linked with those of my parents, grandparents and my many relatives, when a few simple actions had given rise to countless others. What I did in the present had possibly begun a generation previously, with a choice that someone had made. Therefore, just as I am the extension of those who lived in the past, they are also linked with my own future.

I have gazed long at the faces of my ancestors as they were caught and preserved forever by a photographer with his tripod camera and with instructions to stay perfectly sill. I can attempt to interpret their blank expressions, I can note the huge hats of the women, with their tiny constricted waists, or the neat suits and high collars of the men, but I cannot really know them. Only a little of what they did; not what they were.

Sometimes I have known the houses where they lived, changed now but still touched by what used to be. I have held in my hand some of their possessions, a piece of jewellery or a lock of hair and I have seen their final resting places with their names on the head-stones. Did they, I wonder, ever know, as I do, that they were part of history, which passed behind them like a moving backcloth?

I have pieced together the memories, which my parents passed on to me, together with the gleanings of what I overheard and interpreted through the eyes of a child. Unlike modern children, I was not subjected to the flood of specific detail concerning people's problems, their infidelities and motives. Thus I felt secure and I retained an innocence not known today, unclouded by invisible and possibly unbearable pressures. And I am glad it was like that.

My own background was interesting and out of the ordinary. Before I was born, my parents had lived through the First World War and sometimes spoke of it. On each eleventh of November, when the clocks struck eleven we all stopped what we were doing and stood silently, heads bowed. To me the whole world had stopped its spinning and had come to a standstill. When the two minutes of silence were over, a distant cannon boomed and a shiver would go down my back.

'Lest we forget', declared the banners and the wreaths. But we did forget and some of those who had wept for the men who had perished in the Poppy fields, wept again. Another war, another generation. But this time it was to halt the greed and the unbelievable cruelty of a man who had seized whole countries in Europe and was marching into Russia.

When I asked father what the first war had been like, he said that he could not speak of it as a soldier, and, instead of describing the horrors and the bloodshed, he told me an interesting story.

In late 1917, less than six months before the war ended, he had gone to a meeting in a public hall where a psychic lady was speaking to a large audience. He had only one thought in his mind. Would he be called up into the Army where all able-bodied men were increasingly needed? He had no opportunity to ask the lady and got up to leave. He stopped as her voice reached him over the heads of those present.

'That gentleman at the back is disappointed, because I haven't given him a chance to speak. I know that he wants to ask me a question. The answer is 'No'. He won't need to go and he will be a very lucky man!'

He escaped call-up into the Army by only a few weeks and he was indeed a lucky man.

My own teen years marched on towards that second world catastrophe and soon there was to be a repetition of senseless slaughter, of battles fought on land, on sea and in the air, during the bitter winters of Europe and the searing heat of desert and jungle. The Second World War.

It was one Sunday morning, the 3rd of September 1939 when, shocked and horrified, we heard the ominous words of Neville Chamberlain. He said that Britain had demanded an undertaking from Hitler that he would withdraw his military forces from Poland, and went on to say, 'I have to tell you that no such undertaking has been received and consequently this country is at war with Germany'.

My parents and I, sitting in sombre silence round our wireless, received the news without knowing what was in store for all of us. The day before, I had just returned from a holiday and I had my first glimpse of a silver barrage balloon, floating like a whale ready to impede enemy low-flying aircraft. The windows of the train were criss-crossed with sticky tape to prevent flying glass.

The war was not entirely unexpected. We had, for some time, seen indications that something was about to happen and that great upheavals had taken place, especially in Germany, as young people and sometimes whole families, began to appear among us, fleeing from unspeakable horrors. These were the lucky ones and most were Jewish. One girl arrived in my school, silent, lost and thin. She was regarded with kindly curiosity by those of us who could not begin to understand what it was like to lose a home for ever.

On film which came out of Europe, we saw pictures of German youth, teenagers, like ourselves, massed in huge arenas. We saw the swastikas, the black shirts and a small man who ranted and raved like the lunatic that he was.

After that fateful declaration of Sunday morning, things happened quickly. It seemed that, overnight, men and women had been swept away into Army Camps, R.A.F. Stations and Naval bases, while a stalwart band of girls strode off to work on the land, growing food for the National Kitchens. Everybody seemed to set great store by eating carrots. 'You can see in the Blackout if you eat carrots!' they told us. People started Digging for Victory and turned their lawns into potato patches, while the more inventive grew onions on top of their Anderson Air-Raid shelters!

In order that the farmers and the landgirls could have more light for their work, the clocks were changed to give an extra hour. Double Summer Time they called it and somehow it didn't feel right, as if we were interfering in some heavenly plan.

In early September all the street lights were turned off and cars (fewer now) crawled along with their headlights extinguished. My mother, as did everyone else, made black-out curtains for the windows and doors, so that no chink of light would reveal the presence of a city. Air-Raid Wardens patrolled the streets to make sure that all the houses remained windowless and dark.

Town and countryside seemed strangely empty, but the Munition Factories toiled night and day to produce large quantities of guns. Iron railings disappeared in order to make ships and tanks. Hundreds of aluminium pans and kitchen utensils were contributed by housewives for the manufacture of aircraft. My cousin Marion worked in a weaving shed, none stop, producing balloon fabric. In country areas, the signposts were confusingly turned around, because it was thought that any German spies who might be lurking around would thus lose their way!

'You can't go to Blackpool any more!' remarked my mother. 'They've put barbed wire, concrete blocks and old tram lines on the sand to stop the Germans landing. It's like a fort!'

They told us that thirty-eight million gas masks had been delivered from door to door. We hated the things as we carried them in square cardboard boxes, slung clumsily across the chest. The smelled of rubber and disinfectant and I cannot remember that they were ever used.

There grew among us a feeling of unity and sharing and everyone felt the bond of common effort. 'We're all in the same boat', we said, and we showed the two-finger Victory V sign which had been invented by Winston Churchill.

Our new King George and Queen Elizabeth had a daughter, also called Elizabeth who, as a teenager, learned to drive an ambulance and became an officer in the A.T.S.

There was a great deal of what was called 'Make do and mend'. If you were the lucky owner of a pair of silk stockings, ladders were stopped with nail varnish or carefully darned. By the time the American G. I.'s arrived, silk stockings had disappeared and the soldiers gained instant favour if they had the new nylons to give to the girls. There was the myth that nylons would last forever, but of course they never did.

Clothes could only be bought with Coupons and some of my friends went round to elderly Aunts and Grandmas who, by luck or persuasion, might not need theirs. Skirts were short to save material but I read in the newspaper that French girls were making smarter creations by cutting up the curtains! We all wore head-scarves. We also experimented with wooden-soled shoes with a type of hinge which was supposed to allow a foot to bend. But they never bent far enough and so we clumped stiffly along the pavements. Legs were painted a nasty shade of tan with gravy browning (which ran in the rain) and a friend used to draw a line down the back with an eyebrow pencil. Why we did not develop severe chills I cannot imagine, for our stockingless legs stayed cold in the freezing winters. But I doubt if we even noticed!

Our longings for the end of the war seemed to be expressed in the songs we sang. 'We'll meet again on Sunny Day' and 'The White Cliffs of Dover', while the more raucous among us sang 'We'll hang out the washing on the Siegfried Line!'

But a promise of peace seemed to be displayed by the night skies. No longer dazzled by the city lights, we could see the stars again! Up there, towards the South, was Orion with three stars in his belt, where he had been all the time, unchanging. The Plough was sharp and clear overhead and the Pole Star, more brilliant than all the rest, became my symbol of eternity.